WATERSIDE WALKS
In Kent

Lorna Jenner

COUNTRYSIDE BOOKS
Newbury, Berkshire

First published 1999

COUNTRYSIDE BOOKS
3 Catherine Road
Newbury, Berkshire

ISBN 1 85306 572 2

Designed by Graham Whiteman
Cover illustration by Colin Doggett
Photographs by the author
Maps by Huw Williams

Produced through MRM Associates Ltd., Reading
Printed by J. W. Arrowsmith Ltd., Bristol

Contents

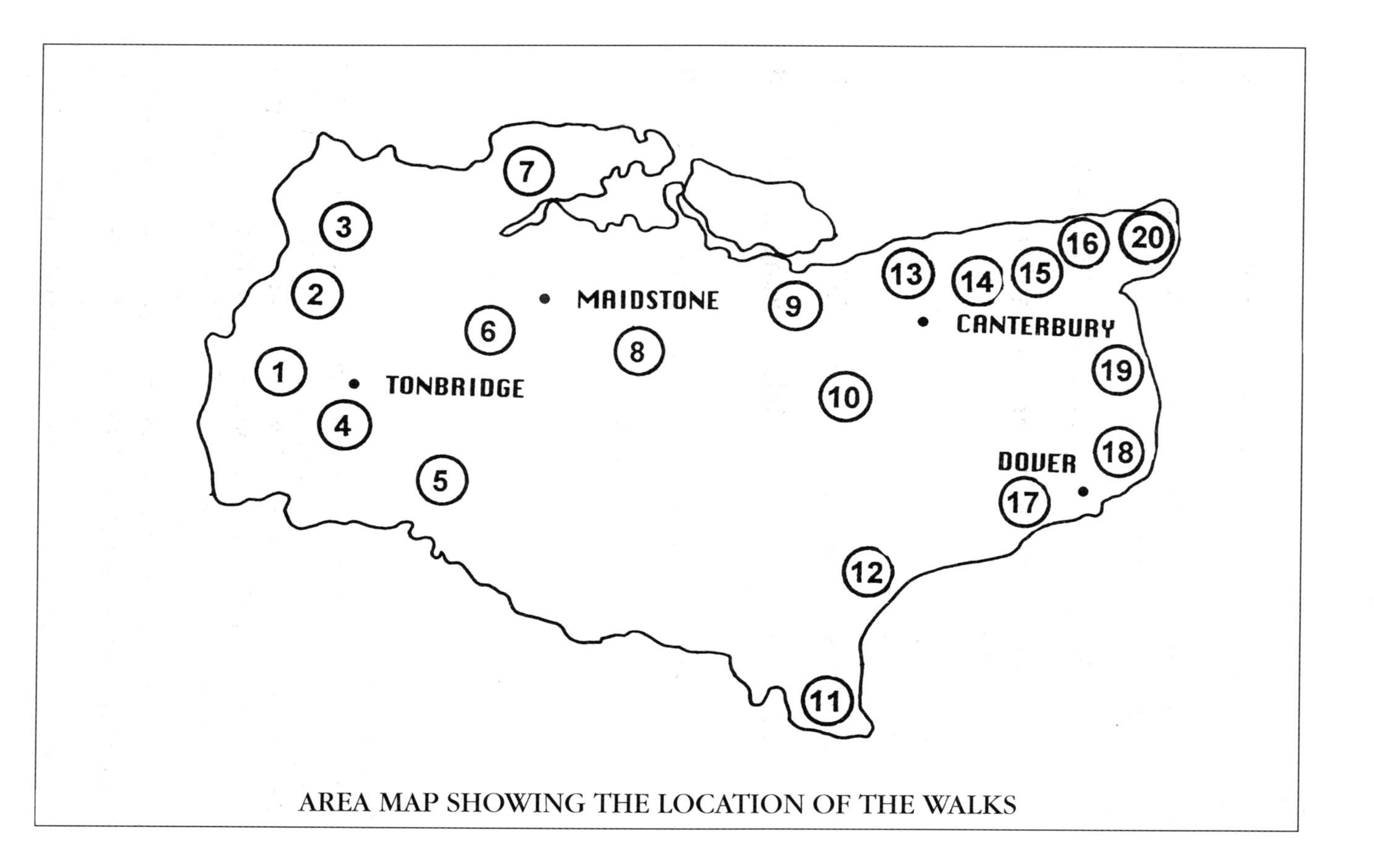

AREA MAP SHOWING THE LOCATION OF THE WALKS

Walk

Publisher's Note

We hope that you obtain considerable enjoyment from this book; great care has been taken in its preparation. Although at the time of publication all routes followed public rights of way or permitted paths, diversion orders can be made and permissions withdrawn.

We cannot of course be held responsible for such diversion orders and any inaccuracies in the text which result from these or any changes to the routes nor any damage which might result from walkers trespassing on private property. We are anxious though that all details covering the walks are kept up to date and would therefore welcome information from readers which would be relevant to future editions.

INTRODUCTION

Kent is a coastal county - bounded on the east and south by the English Channel and by the Thames to the north - and so the sea has had a great influence both on the landscape and the history of the county. As the nearest part of England to the Continent it has always been 'frontier country' - a first landing point for early settlers, invaders and traders, giving it a rich and turbulent history. The Kentish coastline has changed greatly over the past 2,000 years due to the powerful tides that erode away some parts and deposit shingle in others, causing rivers to silt up and change their course. As a result, once thriving medieval ports are now several miles from the sea and large expanses of flat grazing marsh cover former wide estuaries and sea channels.

Reflecting this, many of these walks have links with the sea - bracing clifftop walking along the famous white cliffs; sandy bays edged with chalk rockpools; a vast expanse of shingle; mudflats and wide open estuaries; ancient ports and marshland.

Inland too there is plenty of waterside to explore - riverside walks along the mighty Medway and the meandering Stour; smaller river valleys such as the picturesque Darent, flanked by the downs; and the Teise valley in the rolling High Weald. There are lakes formed from old gravel pits, a reservoir and, perhaps most dramatic of all, a wide moat surrounding one of the most beautiful castles in England!

A pub is described for each walk to add to your day out. In many cases these are cosy historic pubs serving real ales and home-cooked food. The constraints of location have not made such a choice possible on all walks but the larger pubs particularly welcome families and have wide opening hours which may benefit some walkers. The pub details may alter - during the time of writing the landlords changed at three of the pubs - so it may be wise to telephone to confirm opening times. You may be able to leave your car in the pub car park while you walk - if you are a customer - but please ask first. If you opt for roadside parking do be aware of local people and their activities and be careful not to block any exits and entrances.

All the walks are fairly short, between 2½ and 6 miles, and most are suitable for all ages and fitness levels. Where there is a steep climb or descent it is mentioned in the description and also if a walk is particularly suitable for families. I have also mentioned places of interest within easy driving distance of the walk location, to help you plan a full day's outing if you wish.

I am indebted to so many people for their help in writing this book. Thank you to the numerous people who accompanied me on my walks and tried out the pubs! Particular thanks to Denise, Richard and Cathy, Clare and Mike for their hospitality and tolerance as I sat in their houses listening to my dictaphone and typing up notes whilst they plied me with food and drink!

Huw Williams came to the rescue when I realised that my map drawing skills were negligible. Many thanks to him for the hours he spent, not only painstakingly drawing the maps but also enlivening each with illustrations. They are, nevertheless, only sketch maps, provided to show the starting point and main features of the route. I would recommend the use of the Ordnance Survey Landranger sheets or the larger scale Explorer maps for fuller information.

Kent is full of riches for those who take pleasure in waterside walking. I hope you enjoy this small selection of walks and that they may trigger you to explore this stunning county further.

Lorna Jenner

WALK 1

BOUGH BEECH: AROUND THE RESERVOIR

A delightful walk along peaceful footpaths and rural lanes with some good views across Bough Beech Reservoir and opportunities for birdwatching. Many reminders of the area's rich history of iron working, brickmaking and hop growing can be seen en route.

The 15th-century pub at the start of the walk

Walking through this quiet pastoral countryside it is hard to imagine that it has seen so many changes, some slow, others more dramatic. The underlying clay has both shaped the landscape and dictated the landuse. It is impermeable to water and hence the soils are wet and sticky and there is an abundance of streams and ponds. Bricks have been made from this local clay for centuries, particularly in the 17th and 18th centuries, when high quality Kentish tiles and bricks were fashionable building materials. Many of the older buildings on the walk are built from these local bricks.

Farming had always continued alongside the industries but was hampered by the waterlogged soils. When drainage techniques improved during the 19th century, larger scale agriculture gradually took over and hops became an important crop. Round oast houses with their white wooden cowls, once used to dry the hops, dot the landscape around the reservoir.

The 1960s saw the most dramatic change to the landscape when Bough Beech Reservoir was constructed by East Surrey Water Company. A large dam was built, using local clay and the quiet farmed valley was transformed into the large lake that we see today.

The Wheatsheaf in Bough Beech village is a characterful old pub dating from the 15th century. Thought to have been built originally as a hunting lodge for Henry V, it has been added to and altered over the centuries but it has retained its atmosphere with heavy beams, open fires and solid wooden doors. Renowned for its excellent food, there is always plenty of choice including a good range of vegetarian dishes. There is a children's menu and children are welcome in the public bar or the attractive garden which has some play equipment. The pub is open from 11 am to 11 pm on Monday to Saturday and 12 noon to 10.30 pm on Sunday. Food is served all day, although the selection may be more limited between 3 pm and 6 pm.

Telephone: 01732 700254.

- **HOW TO GET THERE:** From Tonbridge take the B2027 through Leigh to Bough Beech village. The Wheatsheaf is on the left just before the railway bridge. From the A25 west of Sevenoaks, take the B2042 to Ide Hill. Beyond Ide Hill take the second left turn, after the Red Lion pub. Continue for about 2 miles to a junction, with a railway bridge straight ahead. Cross the bridge and the pub is opposite.
- **PARKING:** Walkers using the Wheatsheaf may leave their cars in the pub car park. Alternatively, park on the causeway at the northern end of the reservoir and use the pub as a halfway stop, picking up the walk directions between points 4 and 5.
- **LENGTH OF THE WALK:** 6 miles. Maps: OS Landranger 188 or Explorer 147 (GR 488467).

THE WALK

NB: The heavy clay soils can make walking hard work in wet weather so stout shoes or wellingtons are recommended. There are some tall stiles that may prove difficult for the elderly or very young.

1. From the Wheatsheaf turn right and cross the road. After a few yards turn left onto a footpath leading across the railway. Then follow the path diagonally across the field to a woodland shaw in the right hand corner. Cross a stream and follow the path diagonally across a meadow.

2. Climb a stile onto a grassy path edged with thick hedgerows. Follow the path as it runs parallel with the dam, alongside pasture and through pockets of woodland, to a metalled drive leading to Bough Beech Sailing Club.

The round valve tower, which controls the flow of water from the reservoir to the treatment works, is just visible above the dam.

Cross the drive and continue on a footpath across the field, then through a small woodland shaw. Turn left over the next stile and walk along the field edge. Turn right across the field and find a stile in the corner leading down to the road.

The hedgerow is superb in summer with cream dog rose and heavily scented honeysuckle cascading down. The delicate pink flowers of ragged robin at its base indicate the dampness of the soil.

3. Turn right on the road and immediately left over another stile. Walk straight across the field and over another stile onto a quiet lane. Turn left and walk along the lane for about 600 yards.

The thick hedgerows on both sides are hundreds of years old. A hedge can be roughly dated by counting the number of species growing in it over a 100 foot length, each different species equals about 100 years - see how many you can find!

Turn left onto the drive of Bore Place beside the old forge and walk down the drive through the complex of buildings at Bore Place.

There has been a farmstead here since the 13th century. The main house is a Jacobean mansion and there are several fine Tudor timber-framed barns. Common Work Land Trust manage Bore Place for environmental and educational purposes. If you wish to find out more, pick up some leaflets at the reception or explore the grounds using the Field Trail. Handmade bricks are still produced here from the local clay

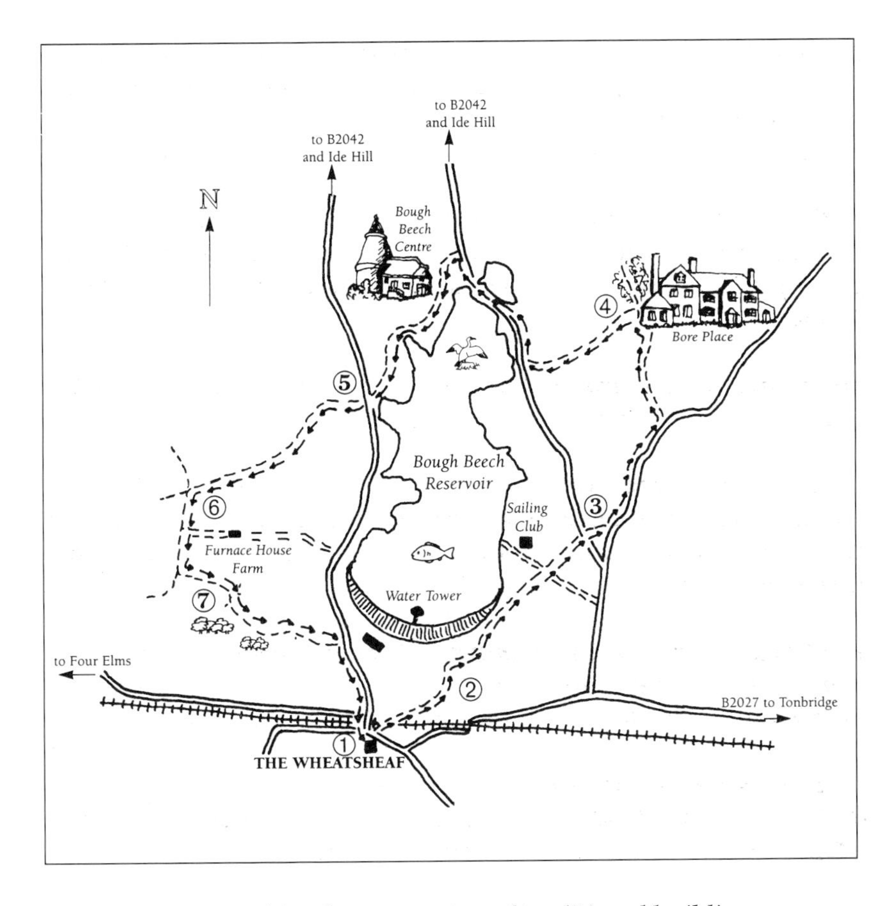

and are in demand for the renovation of traditional buildings.

4. Turn left in front of the brickworks and cross a stile into a large field. Follow the path through crops to a stile in the hedgerow opposite. Then follow the right hand fenceline along the edge of the meadow. Continue straight ahead through a gap in the hedge and follow the path meandering downhill through woodland to the reservoir. Cross the road and turn right to walk on the pavement across the causeway between the main reservoir and a smaller lake.

Good opportunities for birdwatching here - look for cormorants standing on the islands; herons flying slowly overhead; grebes diving for fish; white-beaked coots and smaller red-beaked moorhens. Many less common birds visit on migration.

Beyond the causeway turn left to Bough Beech Centre.

This attractive brick oast house was part of a farm flooded during the reservoir construction. It makes a pleasant spot to picnic even when the centre is closed.

The next section of the walk down to the reservoir is on the Kent Wildlife Trust Nature Trail. Please take care not to disturb the wildlife. Turn left through a gate behind the centre and walk along the field edge. Follow the path diagonally across the next field and across another field to woodland. Continue on the path alongside the woodland until you reach the reservoir edge. Turn right over a stile and walk left diagonally across a field to reach a path running alongside a house to the road.

5. Cross the road and turn right then immediately left into another field. Follow the path along the field edge. At the next field margin the path crosses to the right hand side of the fenceline, then crosses the hedgerow again and leads diagonally across a field towards a stream. Cross the stream in the far corner of the field and then follow the right hand fenceline uphill across two fields.

6. At a footpath crossroads turn left along the crown of the hill. Follow the path along the ridge then turn right onto a driveway. Just before it bears right, take a footpath left and walk downhill across a field.

7. At the bottom of the field cross the stile in the right hand corner into woodland. Follow the meandering path through woods then across a field, keeping woodland and a fence on the right hand side. At the corner of the woodland, bear slightly left across the field, passing a small pond on the left. Then follow the path along the fenceline down to the road. Turn right onto the road and continue for about 500 yards until you reach the bridge over the railway beside the Wheatsheaf pub.

Places of Interest Nearby

Kent Wildlife Trust Centre is open at weekends and on Wednesdays from Easter to October. Its displays include the history of the reservoir area, wildlife and hop farming (telephone: 01622 662012). *Hever Castle*, to the south of Bough Beech, is a beautiful ragstone castle with superb gardens, famous as the home of Anne Boleyn (telephone: 01732 865224).

WALK 2

SHOREHAM: THE DARENT VALLEY

This walk explores one of the prettiest river valleys in Kent. It leads through Shoreham village along the Darent, flanked by pretty cottages, oasts and old mills, then climbs up onto the downs, to give superb views of the village nestling in the valley below.

The bridge over the Darent, at Shoreham

The beauty of the Darent has captivated writers and artists for centuries. Samuel Palmer, the 19th-century landscape artist, lived in Shoreham and described the valley as 'the nooks and dells of paradise'. His dreamy paintings show a rich pastoral landscape framed by the chalk downs. Farming remains important – the fertile soils on the valley bottom growing crops and fattening cattle and the poorer thin, chalky soils of the slopes grazing sheep. The hilltops are wooded as trees grow well in the deeper clay soils which cap the downs.

The river itself was once the lifeblood of the village. It not only provided drinking water and watered livestock and crops but also powered several mills, initially corn and later a paper mill. On the walk you cross several places where the river was diverted to power the mills.

There is no shortage of pubs in Shoreham - this little village boasts five. A long standing favourite of mine is the Royal Oak. A simple late-Victorian building, this friendly hostelry has long been popular with both locals and visitors. It has a wonderful array of well-kept cask bitters: Adnams Best and Broadside, Fuller's London Pride, Brakspear, Shepherd Neame Spitfire and a guest beer. Batemans Dark Mild, Guinness, Heineken and Stella lagers are also served and there are three draught ciders. In addition to a good range of baguettes and sandwiches there is always a choice of specials on the board, including hearty home-cooked, traditional dishes such as bacon hock with mashed potato, pease pudding and carrots. Well-behaved dogs are welcome in the bar and children can eat in the lounge or the small garden. The opening hours are from 11 am to 3 pm and 6 pm to 11 pm on Monday to Friday, all day on Saturday from 10.30 am, and from 12 noon to 3 pm and 7 pm to 10.30 pm on Sunday.

Telephone: 01959 522319.

- **HOW TO GET THERE:** Turn westwards off the A225 between Sevenoaks and Dartford, signed 'Shoreham', about 2 miles north of Otford. Continue into the village, crossing the river, to a T junction. The Royal Oak is on your right. For Filston Lane car park turn left and continue for about 200 yards.
- **PARKING:** There is limited roadside parking on High Street; it would be better to use Filston Lane car park.
- **LENGTH OF THE WALK:** 3 miles. Maps: OS Landranger 188 or Explorer 147 (GR 517616).

THE WALK

1. From the Royal Oak turn left and immediately left down the road leading to the river. Pass the Samuel Palmer School of Art, a fine half-timbered building, on the left opposite the village school and continue across the Darent. Turn left and walk beside the river, past pretty cottages and alongside Water House.

Water House was once the home of Samuel Palmer, who along with fellow artists and writers, including William Blake, was inspired by the beautiful valley.

Continue along the riverside path, with cottage gardens on the opposite bank, to a footbridge.

2. Turn right beside the bridge.

The large white house beyond the fence is an old mill and the Darent divides here to provide the power to drive the mill.

Walk across the fields and at the footpath junction turn right on the path leading back to the village. (You may wish to detour right along the road, round the bend, to explore the church.) To continue the walk, turn left along the road (opposite Shoreham Place) for 200 yards.

3. Turn right onto the path across the golf course, signed 'Darent Valley Path'. Continue across the golf course and cricket square.

4. At a path junction turn right along the track, signed 'Darent Valley Path'. Cross over the Darent on a footbridge and turn left along a bridletrack.

This stream is part of a diverted channel from the main river that once drove the old mill at Filston Hall, an ancient moated manor house that can be glimpsed ahead.

Turn right and walk along Water Lane to Filston Lane. (If a short cut is required, turn right and walk along the road back to the Royal Oak pub.) To continue the full walk, cross the road and climb uphill across two fields on a clear track.

5. Soon after woodland begins on the right hand side turn right onto a woodland track, signed 'Meenfield Wood'.

This is a lovely spot to linger with good views across the valley and a seat to encourage you. The group of oasts of Filston Farm stand out. Oasts were used to dry hops and the large number in this area indicates how important hop growing once was.

Follow this track as it traverses the hillside.

6. Turn right at a path junction when the village is directly below and walk downhill through fields and the recreation ground to the road.

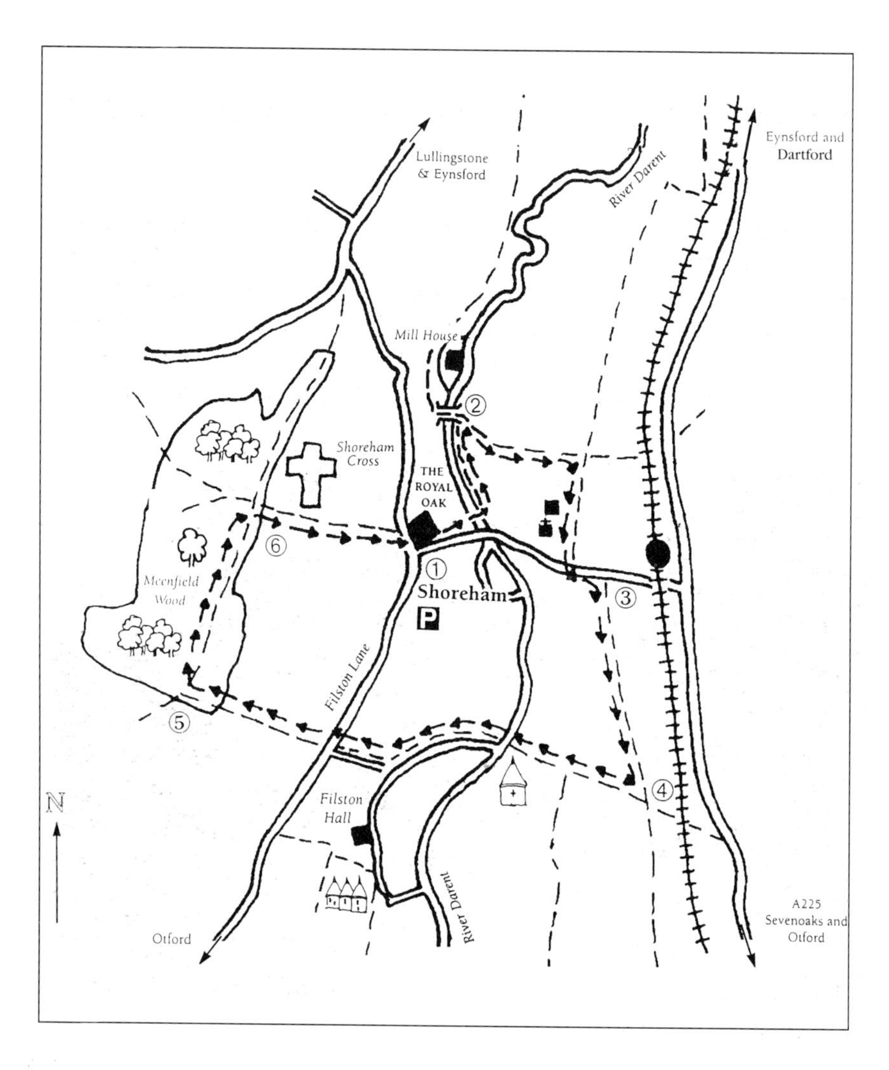

Look back to see the Shoreham Cross cut into the hillside by Shoreham residents as a memorial to local men who died in the First World War.

Turn right along High Street to return to the Royal Oak.

Places of Interest Nearby

Shoreham Countryside Centre will be found in Shoreham Station buildings (telephone: 01959 523098). Just north of the village, the *Lullingstone Park Visitor Centre* houses displays of local wildlife (telephone: 01322 865995).

WALK 3

FARNINGHAM: A DARENTSIDE WALK

Explore elegant Farningham, which once bustled with stagecoaches and carriages, then walk along the banks of the peaceful River Darent to Horton Kirby. Cross the river beside an old mill and over fields back to the river. Then climb uphill, with magnificent wide views of the Thames, to Farningham Woods. Return to Farningham through the quiet beauty of this wonderful old woodland.

The Darent at Farningham

This northern part of the Darent valley, where the downs flatten and the valley widens, has prospered since Roman times owing to its fertility and its close proximity to London. It has always been an important transport corridor - the Romans are thought to have used barges to carry their produce to London via the Darent and the Thames - and it was a natural route for the first roads linking the eastern Channel ports and Maidstone with London. In the 18th century, when the main road was improved and managed by a turnpike trust, Farningham thrived as an overnight stopping point for travellers and most of the houses on the main street date from this period. Railways and more recently motorways have all followed similar routes, although thankfully bypassing the centre of this beautiful village, leaving it quiet and unspoilt.

The Lion is a handsome old inn with an imposing brick Georgian exterior with white pillared doorway and sash windows. Inside, the wooden beams suggest that it may be much older. It was probably refaced with fashionable brick in the coaching era when it was the grandest of the inns in the village. It attracted officers, local gentry and London anglers, drawn by the trout that were then plentiful in the river. Charles Dickens was one such angler, keen to escape the city grime of London. Now part of the Harvester chain, it still retains its historic feel and has a magnificent riverside setting, beside the bridge and mill in the heart of Farningham, with plenty of benches so that you can enjoy the scene outside on fine days.

Both snacks and sandwiches and a more extensive restaurant menu are served. Children are welcome and there is a special children's menu as well as a play area. The opening times are from 11 am to 11 pm, seven days a week, and food is served from 12 noon to 11 pm.

Telephone: 01322 866035.

- **HOW TO GET THERE:** Farningham is approximately 6 miles south of Dartford off the A225. At the roundabout of the A20 and the A225 take the side road signed into the village. Continue along High Street, and the Lion is beside the river.
- **PARKING:** There is a large pub car park and some roadside parking on High Street.
- **LENGTH OF THE WALK:** 3¾ miles. Maps: OS Landranger 177 or Pathfinder 1192 (GR 547672).

THE WALK

1. From the Lion walk down to the riverside and turn left to walk along the river bank, following the Darent Valley Path.

The willow-fringed river is a good place for birdwatching. Ducks and moorhens potter near the pub, undeterred by the visitors and eager for scraps. As it gets quieter the more elusive birds appear – the bobbing grey wagtail with distinctive yellow tummy and long tail, or you may hear the piping 'chee' of the kingfisher or catch a glimpse of its turquoise feathers as its speeds its way above the water.

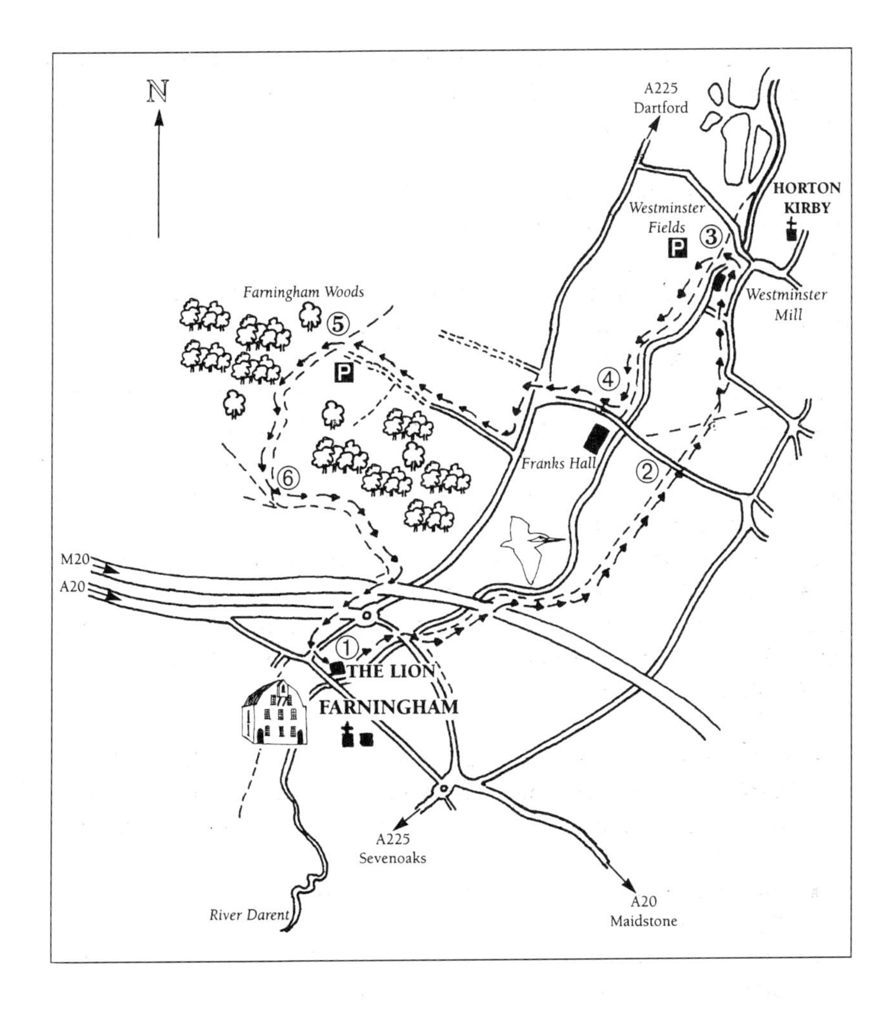

Continue on the riverside path, walking under the A20 bridge. Then cross the river on a small footbridge and turn left to walk along the opposite bank under the huge concrete M20 bridge. Continue along the riverside to a stile then follow the Darent Valley Path right between two fields and left soon after to walk parallel with the river to a lane.

The ornamental conifers in the field give a clue that this was not always farmland - it was the grounds of Franks, a red brick Tudor mansion, and you can glimpse the tall brick chimney pots through the trees just before the lane.

2. Cross the lane and continue on the footpath straight ahead, following the fenceline across two fields. Where the path meets Rays Lane turn left by Royal Oak Cottage and walk along the lane into Horton Kirby village. Where the road curves to the right take a track to the left that crosses the Darent beside a tall brick building onto Westminster Fields. (The village centre with its old church and Court Lodge is worth a detour - continue on the road for a short distance.)

This is Westminster Mill, once a flour mill but later a factory that produced shoelaces and string until 1991. Electricity was originally generated by water from the river and the sluices and weir can still be seen. Westminster Fields is on the site of a large Roman granary. A display panel gives more information.

3. Turn left into the playing field car park and follow the Darent Valley Path across the fields to the river. Walk along the riverside path back to Franks Lane. (For a shorter walk turn left and right soon after, back onto the footpath that retraces your steps back to Farningham.)

4. Turn right up Franks Lane and left onto the main road. Walk along the pavement for about 200 yards, then cross the road and walk up Calfstock Lane. Continue uphill on the lane for ¾ mile to a small car park. From the car park take the broad path into the woods (blue bridleway marker) until you reach a clearly marked path crossroads.

5. Turn left onto a footpath (yellow marker) and walk downhill. Pass several path junctions but continue straight ahead to the bottom of the hill and the woodland edge.

This woodland nature reserve is a quiet oasis away from traffic noise - silent save birdsong and squirrels scuffling about. It is mainly coppiced sweet chestnut interspersed with small open areas and ponds. Interpretive boards give more information about the reserve and the wildlife that lives there.

6. At the woodland edge, cross the stile beside the gate into the field and turn left to skirt along the field edge. At the far corner of the field bear right down the side of the field towards the motorway.

Overlooking the M20 and Farningham village it is easy to see, from

The riverside inn at the start and end of the walk

the shape of the land, why this has always been a main transport route.

At the bottom of the field turn left onto a track. Then turn right opposite houses down steps to the road. Turn right along the pavement, passing under the M20 bridge. At the roundabout cross over to the garage and then turn right down Dartford Road. Turn left at the bottom of the road back onto Farningham High Street. The Lion is 200 yards along on the left.

Places of Interest Nearby

South of Farningham, lies the picturesque village of *Eynsford*, with its ford and attractive jumble of cottages. The ruins of Eynsford Castle, on the riverside opposite the Castle Inn, are always open and are free. Just outside Eynsford are *Lullingstone Roman villa*, the best preserved of the villas that were once dotted along the Darent (telephone: 01322 863467), and *Lullingstone Castle*, an elegant Queen Anne house with earlier Tudor gatehouse (telephone: 01322 862114).

WALK 4

HAYSDEN COUNTRY PARK: RIVERSIDE RAMBLINGS

The walk begins in the quiet hamlet of Lower Haysden, then leads through Haysden Country Park, along the River Medway, into Tonbridge. Historically the area has lots to offer - old canals from an era when water was the cheapest means of transport and the imposing Norman castle built to protect the river crossing.

Barden Lake

The River Medway has brought both prosperity and devastation to this area. Tonbridge was a relatively easy crossing point of the Medway on a main route from the south coast to London and the town gradually developed on the boggy land around the river. Many attempts were made to extend the navigable stretch of the Medway up to Tonbridge and in 1741 it was finally opened. For 150 years the river became the key transport route for the area, bringing increased prosperity until the mid-19th century when the railways gradually took trade away.

Floods devastated the area for centuries. As recently as 1968, Tonbridge town centre was seriously flooded and boats smashed through shop windows on the High Street. Lower Haysden was under several feet of water and in the village pub, the Royal Oak, the water reached over the bar!

This pleasant pub is fairly modern, having replaced an older timbered alehouse. It is a freehouse serving draught Adnams and guest beers, Stella, Beck's and Heineken lagers, Guinness and Strongbow cider. A wide range of food is on offer too. On Monday to Friday from 11 am to 2 pm you will find snacks and basic pub fare such as chips, burgers, French bread sandwiches and ploughman's. On Thursday to Sunday evenings a more varied and extensive menu is available, featuring fresh seafood and Spanish dishes. Both snack and full menus are available on Saturday and Sunday lunchtimes. The pub is open from 11 am to 11 pm on Monday to Saturday and from 12 noon to 10.30 pm on Sunday.

Telephone: 01732 350208.

- **HOW TO GET THERE:** From Tonbridge take the A26 south, over the railway. Turn right past schools and a college and take the first right onto the lane leading to Lower Haysden. The Royal Oak is on the left in the village centre.
- **PARKING:** Walkers using the Royal Oak may leave their cars in the pub car park but please let the landlord know. Alternatively, use the Country Park car parks.
- **LENGTH OF THE WALK:** 3¾ miles. Maps: OS Landranger 188 or Explorer 147 (GR 572457).

THE WALK

1. From the Royal Oak turn left and then right along the road. After approximately 200 yards, where the road bears left, continue straight ahead onto a bridlepath (signed 'Weald Way') into Haysden Country Park. Follow the path as it bears left.

2. Where the bridlepath continues straight ahead, turn right onto a path that crosses over a dry ditch. Continue along the path as it bears left and then right over a wooden footbridge across an old cut.

This remains from James Christie's failed canal scheme. Christie, an entrepreneurial young engineer, sought to extend the navigable stretch of the Medway to Penshurst. The scheme was never completed as Christie was bankrupted and fled to America in 1832.

Follow the path through two kissing gates and at a path junction go straight ahead under the railway bridge. Continue to a path T junction just past Heustamenn Friendship Wood. Turn right, signed to Barden Lake, and immediately left over the footbridge crossing the Medway.

Upstream is the flood barrier, erected in 1981 to prevent further serious flooding. If water levels rise too high upstream of the flood barrier, the excess water will be diverted to flood the park area around Hayesden Water so that Tonbridge is no longer at risk.

Turn right and walk alongside the river for about ½ mile. Ignore a metal bridge on the right and continue straight ahead, crossing two ditches joining from the left on small footbridges.

3. At a T junction, turn right, ignoring the path to Leigh on the left.

These decaying ditches are the remains of a 19th-century canal built to transport gunpowder from the Leigh mills to Tonbridge. The

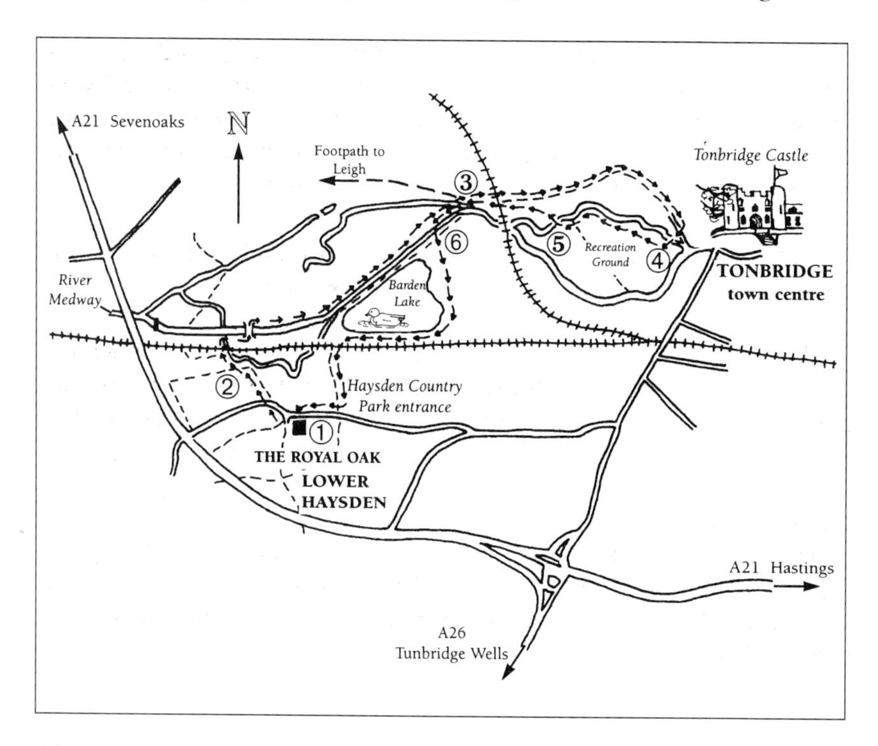

barrels of powder were transferred to larger barges at Tonbridge for the journey along the Medway to ammunition stores at Erith or Chatham. The barges flew a red flag and hulls were sometimes painted bright red to show that they were carrying explosives.

Continue along the waterside path, and follow the path, still the Weald Way, alongside a stream, across playing fields into Tonbridge to the car park in front of the swimming pool. If you want to look at the castle, turn left by the swimming pool and then right along the waterside.

The castle was originally a wooden keep on top of a huge earth mound or motte. It was burned down in 1088 and was gradually rebuilt in stone. The gatehouse, some of the curtain walls and the motte remain, giving an impression of the castle's grandeur in its heyday.

From the swimming pool, turn right and walk down to the river.

4. Cross the river and turn right to follow it.

5. Cross the river once more on a small footbridge and continue straight ahead on the tarmac path to a larger path. Turn left and walk along the path, retracing earlier steps. Walk alongside the river, crossing the footbridges near the Powder Mills junction again, until you reach a larger metal bridge, Lucifer Bridge, on the left.

6. Cross this, and turn right along a small path that pleasantly meanders through woodland down to Barden Lake.

Walk around the lake and follow the path on the far side under the railway bridge. The path to the right leads into the Country Park car park. Take the path bearing left to walk down the main park drive to the road. Turn right and walk along the road, back to the pub.

Places of Interest Nearby

There are play areas at both Tonbridge and Haysden Country Park. *Tonbridge Castle* (telephone: 01732 770929) is worth seeing and there are summer boat trips along the river as well as rowing boats for hire near Big Bridge.

WALK 5

LAMBERHURST: ALONG THE RIVER TEISE

A peaceful walk through the rolling countryside of the Teise valley dotted with hop gardens, orchards and a vineyard. Centred on the picturesque hillside village of Lamberhurst, the walk criss-crosses the Teise and its tributaries many times and from the higher ground there are superb views across the valley.

The Swan, Lamberhurst

The water isn't as obvious as on some of the other walks but the River Teise has played a key part in Lamberhurst's history. The settlement grew up at a crossing point of the river as it lies on the main route from Hastings to London. Tudor iron masters harnessed the waters of the Teise to power the hammers to beat the iron and the walk leads past the remains of this long gone industry. The turnpiking of the main road in the 18th century brought further prosperity as the village became a staging post for traffic travelling between the coast and London.

The Swan is a friendly, homely pub in a peaceful setting away from the busy main road. The building was originally built as two thatched cottages in the 15th century. It has been serving ales since 1720. It was used as a billet for troops during the Napoleonic Wars and later sheltered poor widows and orphans. These days it is a Greene King pub offering IPA, Abbot and Rayments real ales, Strongbow cider and Carling and Kronenbourg lagers on draught. The Swan serves a wide variety of bar snacks including immense 'doorstep sandwiches' and a number of more substantial home-cooked meals such as steak and kidney pudding, ham, egg and chips and Sunday roasts. A children's menu is available and there is a garden.

For opening times telephone: 01892 890200.

- **HOW TO GET THERE:** Lamberhurst is on the A21 south of Tunbridge Wells. Turn off westwards in the village centre onto the B2100. The Swan is on the right just past the vineyard.
- **PARKING:** There is limited parking outside the pub. Better to park on the roadside or in Lamberhurst Vineyard.
- **LENGTH OF THE WALK:** 5 miles. Maps: OS Landranger 188 or Explorer 136 (GR 673356).

THE WALK

1. Turn left in front of the pub and walk along the road past Lamberhurst Vineyard.

The brick oast beside the vineyard is the first of many that you will pass. The round or square oasts are kilns used to dry hops. Most have been converted into houses, a few left to decay, but they indicate that hop growing was once widespread around Lamberhurst.

Turn left onto the main road into the village and climb steps on the left soon afterwards onto a footpath between an orchard and the vineyard.

Lamberhurst is one of England's leading vineyards, producing high quality wines from the grapes grown on the sandy soils of the hillside. Look for the many windbreaks, rows of poplars or tall hurdle fences, that slow down the prevailing winds.

You will see the ruins of Bayham Abbey on the hillside ahead.

Continue straight ahead on the path to a concrete track. Turn left onto the track and right just before a corrugated barn (look for the waymarker at the side of the path as it may be difficult to see the route at harvest time). Walk straight across the field. Continue ahead, crossing to the left hand of the hedgerow and at the end of the hedge walk across the field downhill and slightly to the left to the hedgerow at the bottom (look for the tall conifer on the skyline). Turn right and cross a concealed stile in the hedgerow and follow the narrow path to the left. Cross a metal stile into the grounds of a large house. Go over the drive and take the path straight ahead through the gardens to the greenhouse and garage area.

2. Turn right onto the road and walk carefully along it. Pass a left turn and then turn right along the drive of Furnace Mill.

Hops are still grown on this farm - look for the framework of poles and wire constructed to support the climbing hop plants in the fields.

The attractive cluster of weatherboard and brick buildings at the end of the drive now looks very agricultural, but the large white barn, Furnace Mill, was once a busy iron foundry in the 17th and 18th centuries, famous for casting the railings that once surrounded St Paul's Cathedral. The present Mill House dates from 1722 and was used as a corn mill from 1812 after the forge closed.

Walk past Furnace Mill on the path between an old oasthouse and brick outbuildings. Pass a corrugated barn on the left and follow the track as it bends right, following a dried up, scrub-edged ditch.

This is actually the remains of the canal or leat that carried water from the Teise to the furnace area to drive the hammers for working the iron.

Cross over the Teise. Continue to the road and turn right.

3. Turn right into Hoathly Farm past more oasts and a weatherboard barn. Then take the clearly marked, grassy track in front of the stone farmhouse. Cross a tiny footbridge and walk straight across the field. Follow the clear path diagonally left across the next field to the woodland edge. Turn right and follow the path alongside the wood. Climb the stile and footbridge and follow the path across the meadow.

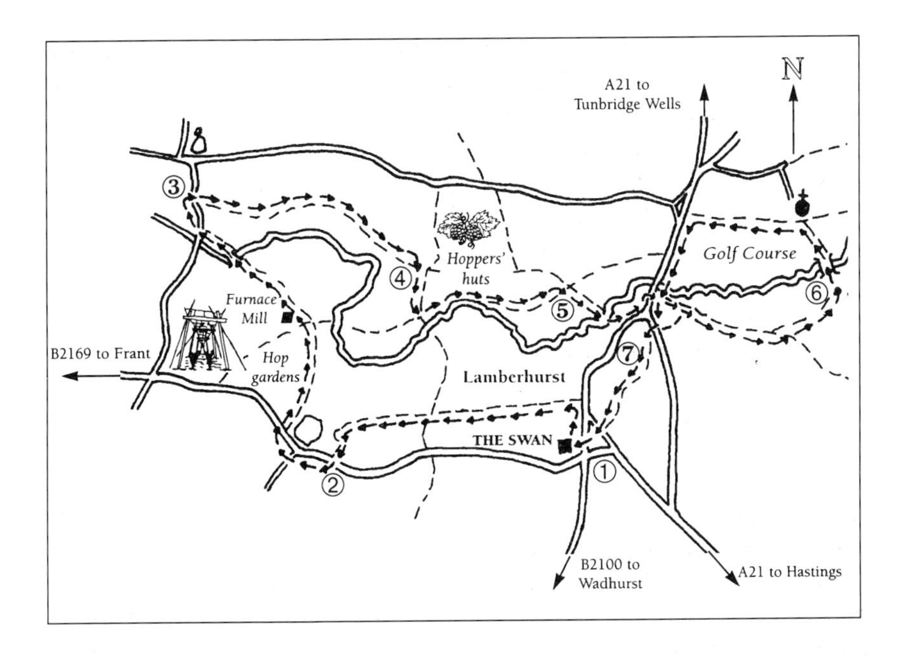

4. At a footpath crossroads (marked 'WC382'), turn right and walk down the fenced track. At the bottom turn left onto the farm track and left again on the path leading alongside the river (don't cross over on the footbridge, keep the river on the right).

The derelict, low brick huts on the left near the river were hop pickers' huts and the small brick building with two chimneys on the right was the cooking shed.

5. Continue on the path to a corrugated barn on the left. Turn right just past the barn onto a small footpath over a stile and walk diagonally left across the field.

Cross the Teise again and follow the path through a pretty garden, back to the road. (For a shorter walk, you could turn right here and follow the road uphill past shops and the vineyard entrance, back to the Swan.) To continue the full route, turn left and walk down to the High Street. Turn left and cross over in front of the Chequers pub.

Two old coaching inns stand on either side of the River Teise - the Chequers and the George and Dragon. The river used to flood regularly, making the road impassable, and the two inns were needed for stranded travellers.

A small section of the railings that were made at the nearby iron furnace for St Paul's Cathedral is set in the wall beside the Chequers.

Walk through the pub garden and across the playing fields with the river to your left. Cross through a stile in the hedge onto the golf course. Take the footpath straight across the golf course to the stile in the fenceline ahead. Cross the stile and a footbridge over a ditch. Turn left and walk along the field edge to a second footbridge crossing the river.

6. Cross the river and take the footpath uphill towards the church. Enter the churchyard and take the path along the left hand wall beside the golf course. At the main road turn left and walk along the pavement above it, back down into the village.

On the right is the handsome village school with elaborate curving Dutch gables, the blacksmith's forge that worked until the early 1990s and the old wheelwright's next door.

Beyond the Chequers keep on the A21 past its junction with the B2100. Beware - this is a dangerous stretch of busy road!

7. Cross the A21 and take the footpath on the right uphill alongside the road. Turn right and cross a small parking area to a residential road. Turn left past houses and then right on a path uphill through fields, past an orchard on the left. Continue uphill on a concrete track between the drives of houses to the road. Cross the road and take the narrow path on the opposite side that meanders to the right around a house (the Casa Pasta restaurant) to the road. Cross the green and turn left to retrace your steps to the vineyard and the Swan.

Places of Interest Nearby

Lamberhurst Vineyard is open to the public for most of the year (telephone: 01892 890844), as are *Owl House Gardens* (telephone: 01892 890230), north-east off the A21 - beautiful gardens surrounding a 16th-century smugglers' cottage.

WALK 6

WEST FARLEIGH AND TESTON: A MEDWAY MEANDER

A gentle scenic walk with a long stretch of riverside walking, an old lock and ancient churches. The return route is across pasture, orchards and a hop garden with views across the Medway valley.

Teston Bridge

From picturesque West Farleigh the walk ambles across fields to Teston Bridge. Nearby Teston Lock was built in 1740 by the Medway Navigation Company as part of their scheme to extend the navigable stretch of the Medway up to Tonbridge. There was subsequently heavy usage for over 150 years, by barges transporting locally produced hops, timber and paper to markets downstream and bringing coal and bricks up to Tonbridge.

The riverside is peaceful nowadays, with shoals of tiny fish darting in the shallow water, luxuriant riverside vegetation and overhanging alders and willows. In summer there are splashes of colour from the spikes of purple loosestrife, yellow spearwort and the distinctive pink flowers of the tall Himalayan balsam.

The walk begins beside the Tickled Trout in West Farleigh, a pleasant whitewashed pub, renowned for its excellent food. Walkers are welcome and may order their food prior to departing on their walk. You can eat in the spacious bar area, outside or in the more formal restaurant. Over 80 dishes are available with a specials board changed every few days. Seafood is a speciality. A good range of meat dishes is served and there are always some vegetarian specials as well as sandwiches, ploughman's and jacket potatoes. Food is served daily from 12 noon to 2 pm and 7 pm to 9.30 pm (9 pm on Sunday). Children are welcome at lunchtimes and in the spacious garden in the evenings and children's meals are available on request. Dog are only allowed in the garden. The choice of draught beers includes Boddingtons and Whitbread, alongside Murphy's, Stella and Heineken lagers and Strongbow cider. A wine list is also available.

Telephone: 01622 812589.

- **HOW TO GET THERE:** Approaching from Maidstone, take the A26 and continue through East Barming. Turn left, signed to the Teston Picnic Site and West Farleigh. Cross the Medway and follow the road uphill into the village. The Tickled Trout is on the right.
- **PARKING:** There is a large pub car park but it gets very busy at weekends. Please ask permission of the landlord if you want to leave your car there while you walk. Alternatively, there is a large pay and display car park at Teston Picnic Site.
- **LENGTH OF THE WALK:** 3¼ miles. Maps: OS Landranger 188 or Explorer 148 (GR 714527).

THE WALK

1. From the pub turn right onto the road and immediately right onto a footpath running alongside the pub garden. The path cuts across the field to the right, to a stile in the hedge in the top right hand corner.

There are lovely views across to Teston church and a grand white stucco building, Barham Court. This elegant building was much admired - William Wilberforce, the politician who fought for the abolition of the slave trade, was a frequent visitor, living at nearby East Farleigh, and wrote that 'for charm of softness and elegance I never beheld a superior to Barham Court'.

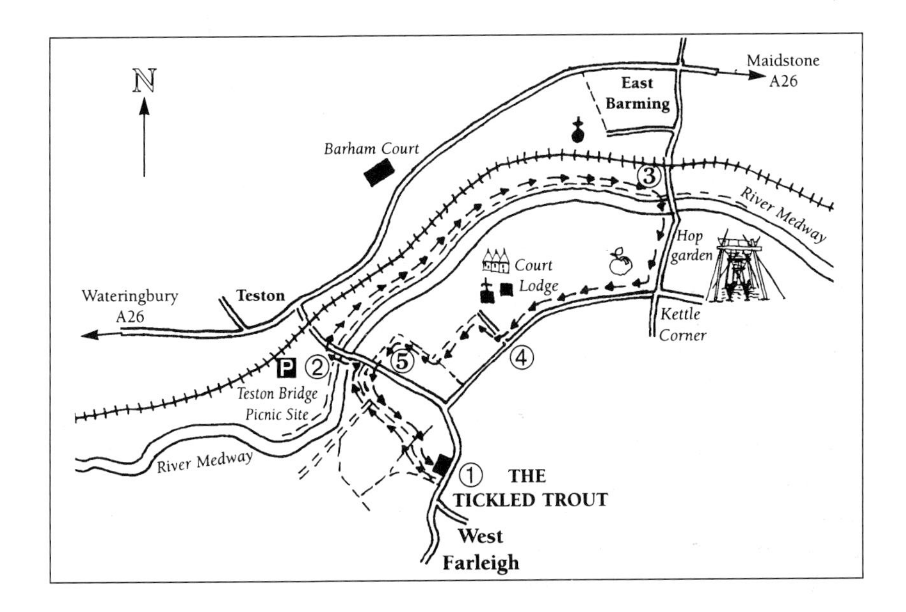

Cross the stile and turn right and then left, following the fenceline (ignore the stile straight ahead) and heading north towards Teston. Climb another stile onto a lane. Turn right and follow the lane to a road. Turn left and walk along the road, crossing the river on the fine stone bridge. To the left along the river is Teston Lock.

The large central arch of the medieval ragstone bridge was rebuilt to provide access for barges as part of the 18th-century improvements to the navigation at a cost of £225 12s 4d!

2. Turn left onto the meadow beside the river at Teston Picnic Site and go left under the bridge, joining the Medway Valley Walk along the riverside. Continue to the next very different bridge, Kettlebridge, a small wooden bridge that is now closed to traffic.

You may admire the huge umbels of giant hogweed along here, but take care not to touch as the sap causes severe blistering.

The slender spire of Barming church stands out on the hillside to the left, separate now from the village of East Barming. At the time of the Domesday survey Barming was divided into East and West, each with their own church, but only one church now remains, separated by orchards from the community it serves.

3. Cross the Medway at Kettlebridge and walk up the lane to the road.

On the left halfway up the lane is a small hop garden. Hops are grown to flavour beer and, at one time, were an important crop in this area until competition from imported hops reduced local production. Hops are climbing plants and, when cultivated, are supported by this intricate network of poles and wire.

Turn right and walk on the pavement alongside the road for about ½ mile.

This stretch of roadside walking is included because of the excellent views it gives of the Medway valley with orchards and hop gardens clothing the slopes and the distinctive white cowls of the round and square oasts that were used for drying the hops.

The handsome Georgian mansion on the right is Court Lodge, framed from the road by two lines of huge chestnut trees, which perhaps once flanked the main drive to this stately house.

4. Turn right down the lane towards West Farleigh church. Turn left onto a path leading along the edge of the cricket pitch and follow the hedgerow alongside another field (yellow arrows on green discs now mark the way). Turn right at the end of the line of tall alder trees and left at the end of the field onto a tree-lined path that runs parallel with the river. Continue on the path to a road.

5. Cross the road just below Teston Bridge onto the lane opposite. Then turn left onto the footpath and retrace your steps across the fields back to the Tickled Trout.

Places of Interest Nearby

Along the Medway, beyond Maidstone, is the *Museum of Kent Life*, Cobtree, Maidstone (telephone: 01622 763936). This living museum recreates the sights, sounds and smells of rural Kent life. It would be an ideal visit for those interested in the orchard and hop gardens seen on this walk.

WALK 7

UPNOR: BEACHCOMBING AND BOATBUILDING

A fascinating walk following the Medway as it meanders out to join the Thames estuary. From the little village of Lower Upnor, a 19th-century holiday resort that now has a jumble of chandlers' shops, marinas and waterside pubs, the walk climbs through woodland and along the higher ground to Hoo St Werburgh giving commanding views of the estuary. Walk back along the shoreline, watching the bustle of boats on the river. Much of the route follows the Saxon Shore Way (SSW) and is clearly waymarked.

The Medway estuary

The Medway estuary has always been important for shipping. The Tudor dockyard at Chatham built warships and large numbers were often moored in the river. Hence it was frequently the target for attack during the era of sea warfare. On the walk you can see the remains of several fortresses that were built to protect the English fleet and dockyards. Threats of invasion have long since gone but the river remains busy with craft, largely sailing dinghies and yachts for pleasure.

The walk starts and finishes near the Ship in Lower Upnor. This is a friendly, fairly modern pub beside the river, built on the site of an earlier pub, the Smack, that burned down in 1920. It offers a wide range of home-cooked food and in the evening the menu specialises in seafood, including unusual dishes such as skate in black butter sauce, swordfish and halibut. Home-made pies are usually on offer, vegetarians are well catered for and a traditional Sunday lunch is served. In addition there is a good variety of snacks and basket meals. A children's menu is available and there is also a pleasant garden. Dogs are welcome on a lead in the bar. Real ales include Crows Nest, a locally brewed beer, Speckled Hen, Spitfire and Courage Best. Kronenbourg and Hofmeister lager are on draught and French wine can be bought by the glass.

The pub is open all day from 11 am to 11 pm on Monday to Saturday and from 12 noon to 10.30 pm on Sunday. Food is served every day from May to September; during the winter it is every lunchtime and on Friday, Saturday and Sunday evenings (phone to confirm).

Telephone: 01634 290553.

- **HOW TO GET THERE:** From the roundabout on the A228 between Strood and Grain (near Wainscott) take the road signed to Upnor. Take the first left and follow the road to Lower Upnor. The Ship is on the left and the car park is at the end of the road on the left.
- **PARKING:** There is a large car park beside the Ventura Centre at the northern end of the village. Some roadside parking may also be available.
- **LENGTH OF THE WALK:** 4½ miles. Maps: OS Landranger 178 or Explorer 163 (GR 760711).

THE WALK

NB: The return route leads along the shoreline for 1¼ miles - check the tide times before planning your walk as this section can be impassable for an hour at either side of high tide. Telephone Riverside Services Management: 01795 561234.

1. Cross the road in front of the pub and turn left to walk on the path alongside the river.

2. Beside the Ventura Centre, turn left and follow the path that climbs uphill through woods, signed 'Saxon Shore Way'. Turn right beside wooden steps and then left after the second set, following the path through woodland until you reach a track. Continue walking uphill on the track and continue uphill where it becomes a road.

There are good views from the gap in the trees back to Rochester, with the M2 bridge on the skyline. Nearer is Upnor Castle, built in the reign of Elizabeth I to defend the warships that lay at anchor in the Medway.

3. At the road junction turn right onto a narrow lane and continue straight on along a narrow footpath behind houses. Pass an old orchard on the left and continue straight ahead along a wider track with fields on the right and an orchard on the left.

The tall pollarded poplars on the right hand fenceline backing onto houses were probably planted to shelter orchards.

Ignore a track off to the left and continue ahead towards Cockham Farm. Keep going straight ahead along the track on the clearly marked footpath (SSW), ignoring other tracks at the crossroads before the farm. Pass the farm buildings on the left and Hoo Lodge on the right. Continue on the track over the brow of the hill and then descend.

Wide views open out across the flat marshland. In the foreground is the spire of Hoo church, ahead is Kingsnorth Power Station and the Isle of Grain.

4. At the bottom of the hill turn left alongside housing along the field edge then right onto a small path leading into the churchyard. Walk through the churchyard to the road on the far side. Turn left along the road for 100 yards.

The spire of this old stone church is covered with wooden shingles, a common roofing material until tiles became widely available.

5. Cross the road and turn right along the lane signed to the Country House Nursing Home. At the end of the lane turn right in front of the nursing home and follow the path down to the shore.

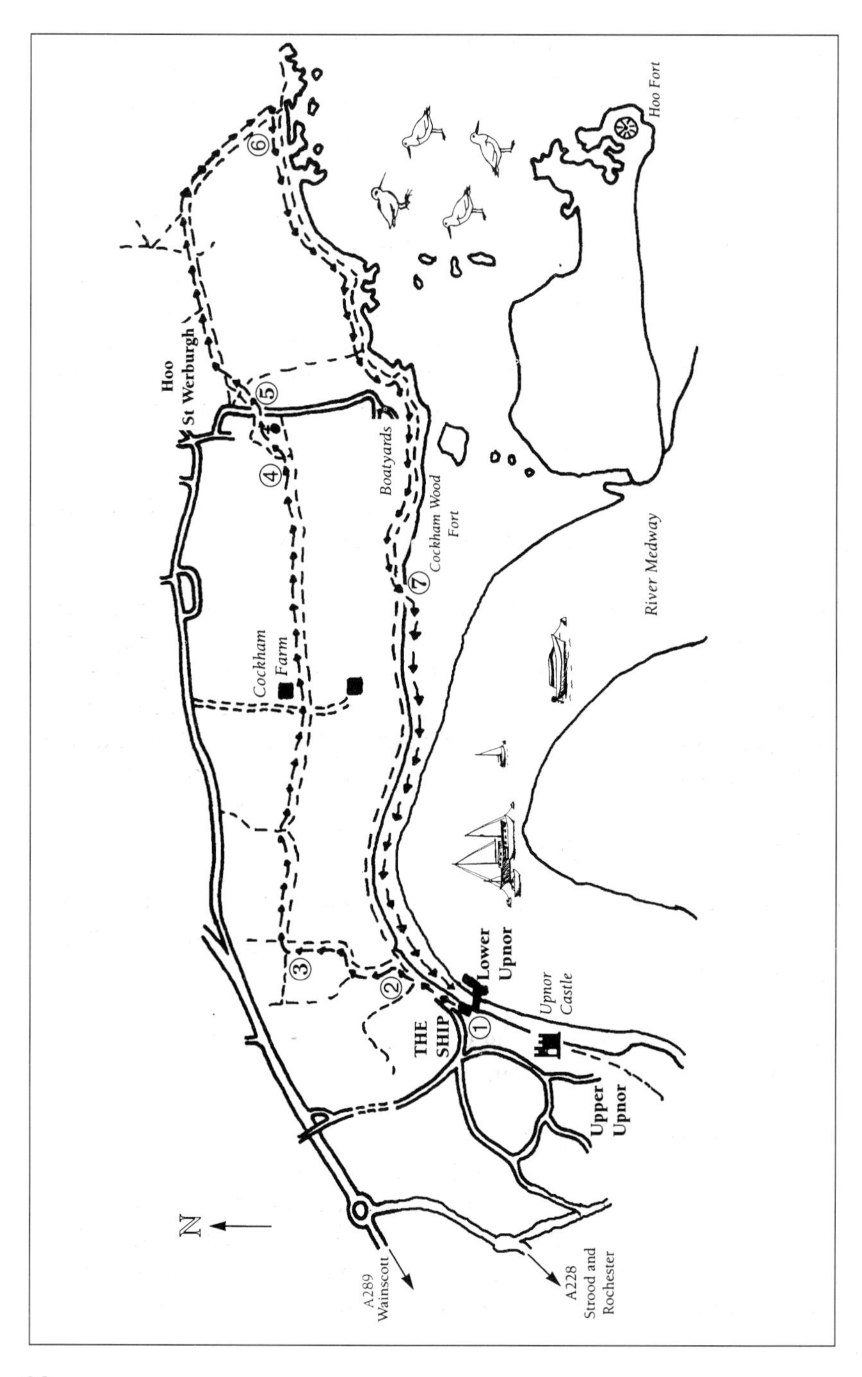
Hoo Fort
Hoo St Werburgh
Boatyards
Cockham Wood Fort
River Medway
Cockham Farm
Lower Upnor
Upnor Castle
THE SHIP
Upper Upnor
N
A289 Wainscott
A228 Strood and Rochester
1
2
3
4
5
6
7

Superb views - notice the derelict Hoo Fort, built on an island in the middle of the river to protect the Medway estuary from the threat of invasion in the 19th century. It was never fully manned with guns as the weight would have made the island sink in the mud.

6. Turn right and walk along the shoreline beside the saltmarsh. From here the route follows the Saxon Shore Way markers all the way back to Lower Upnor. Cross the stile by the brick shed wall and walk straight ahead to the boatyards. Take the narrow path running alongside Whitton Marine which threads its way between the boatyards and industrial workshops. Walk alongside the Hundred of Hoo Sailing Club. At the junction with Cedar Lane take the small path to the left between boatyards and small bungalows/mobile homes.

This is still very much a working area with workshops and industrial units interspersed with the boatyards.

Follow the waymarked path as it weaves close to the riverside between the mobile homes and bungalows with works on the right and boatyards and sailing clubs on the left; it is clearly waymarked 'SSW'. Beyond the Peninsula Press works on the right, go through the metal kissing gate and walk along the clear path to the shore with a car park on the right and mooring for barges and larger boats on the left.

7. Walk along the shoreline back towards Lower Upnor.

The collapsing brick structure is the remains of Cockham Wood Fort, built to protect the Chatham dockyard following a serious Dutch raid in 1667.

Walk past the Wilsonian Sailing Club, on the right, and the yacht club car park, back to Lower Upnor.

Places of Interest Nearby

Situated on the Medway just south of Lower Upnor, *Upnor Castle* is a well preserved Tudor gunfort (telephone: 01634 718742). *Rochester* itself on the opposite banks of the Medway is well worth a visit with its Dickens' connections and imposing Norman castle. Telephone the Tourist Information Centre for further details (01634 843666).

WALK 8

LEEDS AND BROOMFIELD: A CASTLE MOAT WALK

The water here is of a most dramatic type - a huge moat surrounding an imposing Norman castle whose tall walls rise formidably from the water. A short walk leads from the historic village of Leeds, through the grounds of Leeds Castle to Broomfield village and returns along a footpath above the castle grounds.

Leeds Castle

Leeds village is often overlooked by visitors rushing to visit the castle itself. It actually predates the castle and was thriving by Anglo Saxon times, and in the Domesday Book was recorded as having a vineyard, a mill on the banks of the Len and a church. The Manor of Leeds was granted to Robert de Crevecouer, one of William the Conqueror's barons, for his role in the Battle of Hastings. At that time the Saxons far outnumbered the conquering Normans and the magnificent stone castle, built on two islands in a lake, was begun in 1119 as a show of Norman strength.

The castle's most glorious years were perhaps those when it was owned by medieval and Tudor kings. It was an ideal stopping point on royal visits to the Continent as it was one day's ride from London and the coast. Henry VIII was the most famous owner, who spent enormous sums of money enlarging and beautifying it. The castle was added to many times over the centuries, resulting in the beautiful mellow stone building that remains today. Its final private owner was Lady Baillie who painstakingly restored it and founded the Leeds Castle Foundation to ensure that it is preserved for ever.

The George is an attractive tile hung and brick coaching inn in the heart of the village. It is roofed with old handmade red Kentish tiles that have a distinctive uneven appearance. Look for the wonderful catslide roof at the back. Shepherd Neame ales are served alongside Oranjeboom and Hürlimann lagers and a small selection of wines. A good range of food is on offer and the menu changes regularly. Home-cooked specials such as beef and Guinness or farmhouse chicken pies, Cajun chicken or honey roast ham are always available in addition to sandwiches, salads and jacket potatoes, plenty of puddings and tea and coffee. Children are welcome and can choose from a children's menu or opt for small portions of adult meals. The garden is pleasant with lovely views of the old roofs and chimneys. The opening hours are from 11 am to 11 pm and food is served every day during opening hours.

Telephone: 01622 861314.

- **HOW TO GET THERE:** From the A20 between Maidstone and Ashford turn southwards at the roundabout by the Great Danes Hotel onto the B2163, signed to Leeds Castle. Continue past the castle entrance into Leeds. The George is in the middle of the village.
- **PARKING:** Walkers using the George may leave their cars in the pub car park but please let the landlord know. Alternatively, there is limited parking in the village.
- **LENGTH OF THE WALK:** 3 miles. Maps: OS Landranger 188 or Explorer 148 (GR 824533).

THE WALK

NB: Please note that you do not have access to the castle and must remain on the footpath at all times.

1. From the pub turn right and walk along the road uphill to the church.

The ancient church still has many Norman features. Look for 'tufa' which looks like pumice and comes from the bed of chalk streams. It was frequently used by the Normans and can be clearly seen on the tower.

Walk through the churchyard and continue straight ahead across a field to join the road beside the 15th-century Battel Hall. Cross the road and walk straight ahead into the grounds of Leeds Castle. Cross the cricket green.

2. Walk diagonally right across the field to a yellow waymarker in the middle of the field. Keep on the mown path leading towards the main drive. Continue on a tarmacked drive over a cattle grid and into Leeds Castle. Follow the drive down towards the lake and castle.

In front of the castle is a heavily fortified mill, built on the site of the original Saxon mill.

In front of the castle bear right along a tarmacked path (footpath waymarker) towards the courtyard complex and then left, following a path leading alongside the moat opposite the castle. Follow this drive out of the grounds.

3. Turn right onto a quiet lane and follow it for approximately ½ mile into Broomfield.

This pretty hamlet, with its simple stone church set up on a hillside, was also under the influence of the castle at one time. The upkeep of St Mary's Well in front of the church was paid for by the Lady of Leeds Castle in the 16th century. The church itself came within the orbit of Leeds Priory founded at the same time as the castle.

Walk uphill through the village.

The lane is lined with attractive cottages and houses of varying age. Opposite the church are Barracks Cottages, a lovely mixture of brickwork and stone, with ornate details - decorative galleting, tiny stones in the mortar surrounding each large stone block, and pretty roundheaded windows with leaded lights. Higher up the hill on the left is Church Farmhouse, dating from 1400, white weatherboard and brick with a mellow red tile roof.

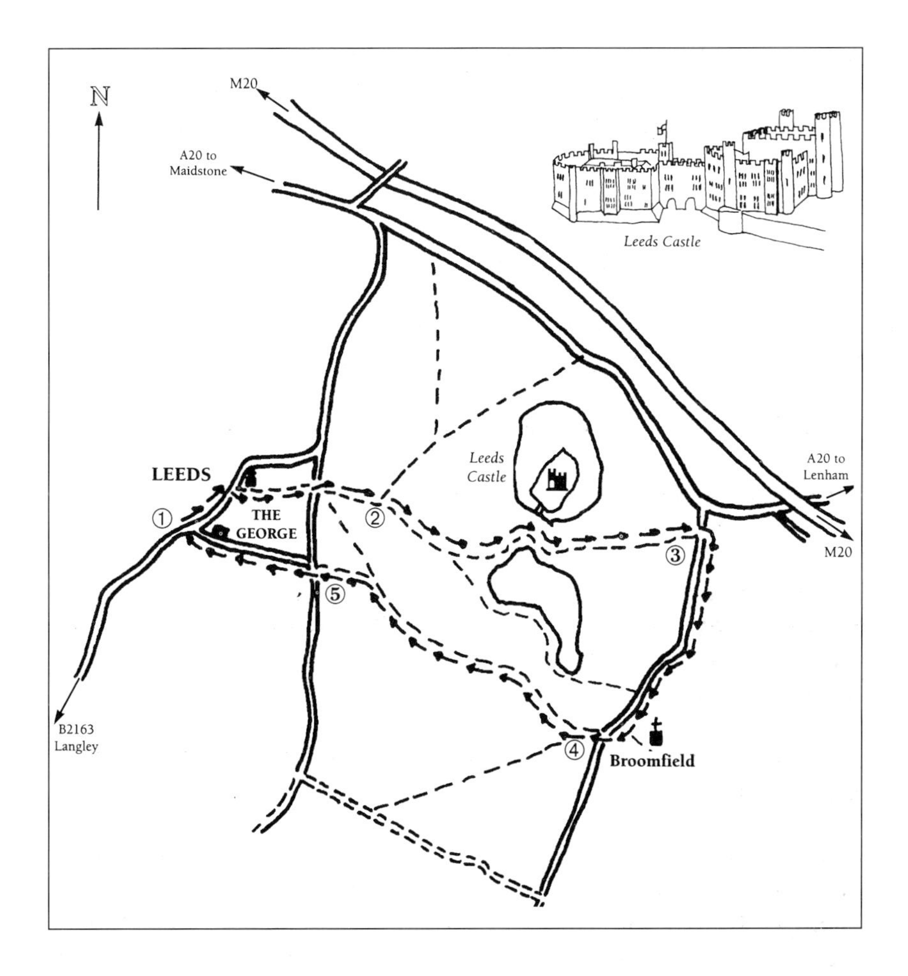

4. Turn right onto a footpath past Church Farmhouse. Where the path forks at the field edge, bear right and follow this path alongside a large field on the left and a hedgerow on the right. Beyond the field follow a clearly mown grassy path through young trees. Go through a gate and walk along the right hand edge of another field to a stile that leads back into the castle grounds (ignore a Shepherd Neame waymarker indicating diagonally across to the cricket ground). Turn left over a stile and walk alongside the hedgerow to meet the drive at the entrance to the castle grounds.

5. Leave the castle grounds and walk downhill on the lane. Go straight across the crossroads and continue downhill on the lane to join the road in Leeds with the George pub on the right.

WALK 9

FAVERSHAM: CREEKS, BOATS AND BREWERS

A refreshing walk that takes you from the quayside and jetties of old Faversham, out across the silent grazing marshes to the estuary where Faversham Creek joins forces with Oare Creek as they flow to meet the Thames. A fascinating area, peppered with remnants of former industries and sailing boats and a haven for wetland birds and flowers.

The Shipwright's Arms, Faversham

Like so many towns on the North Kent coast, Faversham's history is inextricably linked with the sea. The town was a thriving medieval and Tudor Cinque Port, providing warships for Tudor kings and earning the title of 'The King's Port'. Its commercial heyday was the 19th century when the creek was improved and wharves were built so that large ships could get right up to the town. Shipbuilding grew alongside the increased trade and also brickworks, gunpowder mills and oyster fisheries. All have since declined as the creek slowly silted up and alternative transport took over but it is still navigable to small craft and remains popular for sailing.

The distinctive smell of malt and hops pervades the air near the town, reminding us that one old industry is still thriving. Shepherd Neame is Britain's oldest brewery, established here around 300 years ago. The modern brewery is built on the original site and still uses local spring water, from the artesian wells below, and locally grown hops.

There is a choice of two pubs on this walk. The starting point is beside the Albion (telephone: 01795 591411) which is on the creekside in Faversham itself. This is an attractive weatherboard inn serving Shepherd Neame ales. The opening times are from 11 am to 3 pm and 6.30 pm to 11 pm during the week (evening opening from 6 pm on Friday and Saturday) and from 12 noon to 3 pm and 7 pm to 10.30 pm on Sunday. Bar snacks and more substantial meals are available.

For a more isolated maritime feel, the Shipwright's Arms out on the estuary, halfway through the walk, is perfect. This white weatherboard pub got its name from the barge building yard that was situated here at the confluence of Faversham and Oare Creeks. Records show that at least one of the landlords, Thomas Madams, in 1847, was also a barge builder. It is still surrounded by boatyards although their main trade is now yachts and dinghies sailed for pleasure rather than the working boats of bygone days. Low-ceilinged and beamed, the pub still retains much of its original character. Food is hearty and generous portioned. Snacks such as garlic bread, chips and melted cheese, sandwiches and baked potatoes or more substantial meals such as Yorkshire ham or butcher's sausage, egg and chips are available. Huge cooked breakfasts are served before 1 pm and a speciality is home-cooked savoury pastry puddings including lamb and mint, steak and kidney and chicken and leek. Children are well catered for with a family room, large garden and children's meals. The pub dog is particularly friendly both to children and other dogs!

This is a freehouse with a good reputation for its real ales served from the barrel, including Shepherd Neame and Goacher's Mild from Maidstone. There are also guest beers, usually nationally known names such as Adnams or Fuller's London Pride. Also Shepherd Neame's Oranjeboom and Hürlimann lagers and local Pawley Farm cider. The Shipwright's Arms is open from 11 am to 11 pm on Monday to Saturday and from 12 noon to 10.30 pm on Sunday. Food is served from 12 noon to 3 pm and 7 pm to 9 pm every day.

Telephone: 01795 590088.

- **HOW TO GET THERE:** From the A2, Sittingbourne direction, turn left to Faversham. Follow this road around Faversham town centre, turn left past the Shepherd Neame brewery, cross the river and follow the road to the right. Turn right into Lower Brent car park beside the Albion pub.
- **PARKING:** Use the public car park at Lower Brent. There is limited parking near the Shipwright's Arms at Hollowshore.
- **LENGTH OF THE WALK:** 3½ miles. Maps: OS Landranger 178 or Explorer 149 (GR 016618).

THE WALK

1. Turn left from the car park and walk along the quayside past the Albion and follow the Saxon Shore Way along the creekside.

This low weatherboard building is typical of many that would have stood on both sides of the creek at one time. A look up and down the creek tells much of past eras - the old warehouses opposite, the occasional wooden Thames barge dotted amongst the moored modern boats. The tall chimneys of the modern brewery can be clearly seen and beyond that the distinctive slender spire of Faversham church.

2. Turn left away from the creek alongside some modern brown weatherboard flats and then go right behind the flats. At the end of the path reach the road by City Electrical Factors Limited. Continue straight ahead onto the road opposite the works entrance and then turn immediately right onto the footpath between houses and the factory wall as the road bears left. Follow this path around the back of the industrial units. At a path junction turn right and walk back down to the creekside.

At one time dockyards edged this creek, near the present industrial units, firstly White's yard where sailing barges were repaired and then a much larger yard, opened in 1917, which built thousands of lighters, coasters, tugs and trawlers until 1970.

3. Turn left and walk along the raised path along the creekside.

The rough grassland was the site of Perry's brickfield, one of the many brickfields that ringed Faversham in the 19th century, using

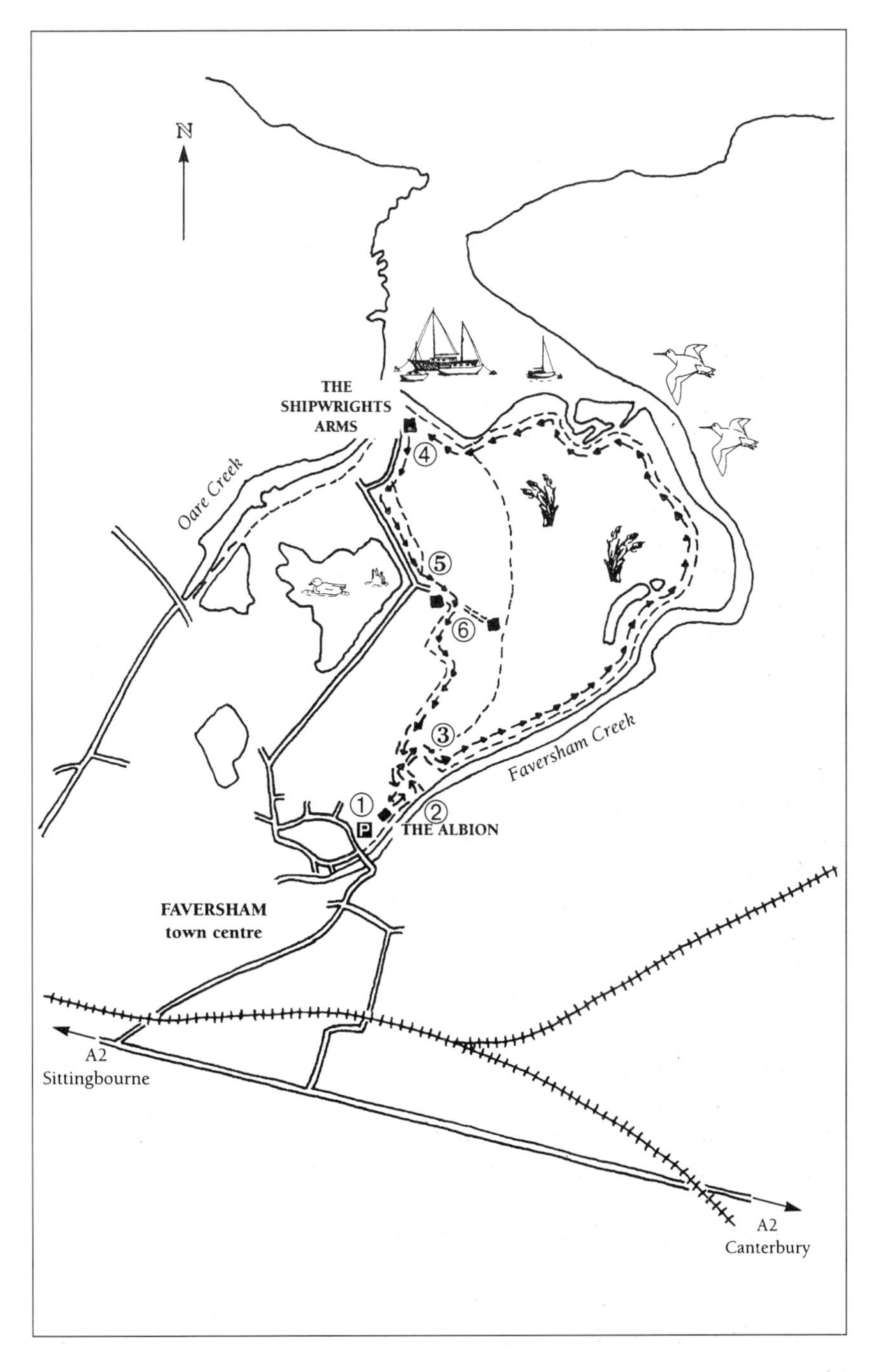
N
THE SHIPWRIGHTS ARMS
Oare Creek
4
5
6
3
1
2
THE ALBION
Faversham Creek
FAVERSHAM
town centre
A2
Sittingbourne
A2
Canterbury

the local clay to make high quality bricks. Many parts of Victorian South London are built from Faversham bricks and, in its heyday, the creek would have been busy with sailing barges loading bricks from its wharves. Look for the old Oyster Bay House on the opposite bank, all that now remains of the once thriving oyster dredging industry.

Follow the path along the raised earthen seawall as it follows the curving creek out to the estuary.

The earthen seawall that you walk along and the network of drainage ditches on the grazing marsh were constructed centuries ago both to reclaim the silt enriched marsh and to prevent flooding.

The mudflats, exposed when the tide is out, attract large numbers of wading birds to feed on the worms and molluscs that live in the mud. Look out for the distinctive white and black osytercatcher with its orange beak, the large shelduck resting on the mud and scurrying flocks of smaller waders.

Looking ahead towards Sheppey, the views are wide and open, broken up only by rows of poplars, masts of ships and occasional tall chimneys.

4. Turn left and climb down from the seawall in front of the Shipwright's Arms pub. Walk past the pub and continue along the quiet lane as it bears left. Pass a small lake on the right.

5. Where the road bears right continue straight ahead along Ham Farm drive.

6. Turn right beyond the farmhouse and follow the path behind the house, across the fields, back to the footpath junction by the industrial estate. Rejoin the path to walk behind the industrial estate and the modern flats to rejoin the creek and walk back to the car park.

Places of Interest Nearby

The centre of this historic town is well worth exploration. The *Fleur de Lis Heritage Centre* (telephone: 01795 534542) on Preston Street is a good starting point as it's packed with leaflets on the town and surrounding area. *Brogdale*, just outside Faversham, off the A2, is home to the national fruit collection and there are regular orchard tours and events (telephone: 01795 535286).

WALK 10

CHILHAM: A RIVER AND LAKES CIRCUIT

A pleasant walk from the exceptionally pretty square at Chilham to Chilham Lakes, past the tall white mill and across fields beside riverside woodland. Walk back along a scenic, meandering path between the River Stour and the lakes, giving plenty of opportunity to watch wildlife and enjoy the tranquil waterside.

The White Horse, Chilham

Chilham is a historic hilltop village with an old square of half-timbered and tile hung cottages flanked by a grand Jacobean mansion at one end and the White Horse pub and old flint church at the other. Narrow lanes lined with cottages descend from each corner.

The cosy White Horse dates from the Tudor period, like much of the village. Its interior retains a historic feel with beams and a huge inglenook fireplace which holds a roaring fire in the winter months. Flowers and the local Swale Brewery's Kentish Pride real ales are offered, also draught Strongbow cider, Murphy's, Heineken and Stella lagers and a good range of wines are available by the glass. The interesting range of meals includes tarragon salmon and lemon ginger chicken, and there are daily specials such as lamb jalfrezi or pork and apple sausage casserole. Ploughman's and jacket potatoes are also served but not sandwiches. The opening hours are from 11 am to 11 pm on Monday to Saturday and 12 noon to 10.30 pm on Sunday and food is served from 12 noon to 2.30 pm and 7 pm to 9.30 pm (no food on Sunday evenings).

Telephone: 01227 730355.

- **HOW TO GET THERE:** Turn westwards off the A28 south of Canterbury onto the A252 and then go left, signed 'Chilham', to reach the village square.
- **PARKING:** There is some parking in the square in front of the pub. A larger car park is down the hill beyond the Copper Kettle tearooms or there is a small pay and display car park by Chilham Mill (you would then start the walk at point 3).
- **LENGTH OF THE WALK** 3 miles. Maps: OS Landranger 179 or Explorer 137 (GR 068536).

THE WALK

1. From the pub turn left past the church and leave the square down a road lined with an attractive jumble of shops and cottages.

Chilham was of great importance historically as it was in a strategic position on top of the downs overlooking Canterbury. The bells resound across the square from the squat tower of the 13th-century church. The old yew tree in the churchyard predates the church, being well over a thousand years old.

At the bottom of the hill turn left along the road out of the village. Ignore the first turning on the right into housing and continue to the main road junction.

2. Turn right along the sliproad (beware – no footpath for a short section!) and cross the A28. Continue along the narrow lane straight ahead, following Stour Valley Walk signs, over the level crossing and along the Mid Kent Water drive. Cross the Stour and walk on the path in front of Chilham Mill.

This is an ideal location for a mill where the river is wide with a good flow of water and there has been a water mill on this site for centuries. One is recorded in the Domesday Book and at one time it was owned by Henry VIII. The present mill was built in the 19th century and was known as a 'French mill' perhaps due to the Caen stone imported from Normandy for its building. It was carefully restored by Mid Kent Water in the 1960s and is now used as a pumping station. The mill stands on an island between the main river and the mill leat that was built to divert water to drive the mill.

3. Beyond the mill turn left in front of a cottage and walk on the path alongside the river. Where the path forks, take the lower path to the left (the path to the right leads up Julliberie Downs, giving good views back to the valley).

One of the earliest battles between the invading Romans and the Britons took place nearby and it is thought that Julliberie Downs takes its name from Julius Laberius, one of Caesar's captains who died fighting here and is reputedly buried on the hillside above.

Walk along the field edge beside tall overhanging trees on the left.

The wet woodland on the left is mainly osier willow and provides homes for many birds and animals.

At the gate turn right along the hedgerow and then left over a stile (very overgrown with vegetation) to follow the hedgerow along. Cross the stile from the field into the lane.

4. Turn left along the lane in front of Stile Farm. At the road junction turn left onto the road that crosses over the Stour.

5. Just over the river turn left onto the Chilham Lakes Nature Walk that leads back on a path between the river and the lake.

The Chilham Lakes Nature Walk leads alongside the flooded gravel pits that are now managed by Mid Kent Water. It is interesting at all times of year - colourful yellow flag iris and marsh marigold in the spring; swans with cygnets and dragonflies in summer; brown furry seedheads of reedmace and the autumn colours; the many ducks and other waterbirds that gather to spend winter here.

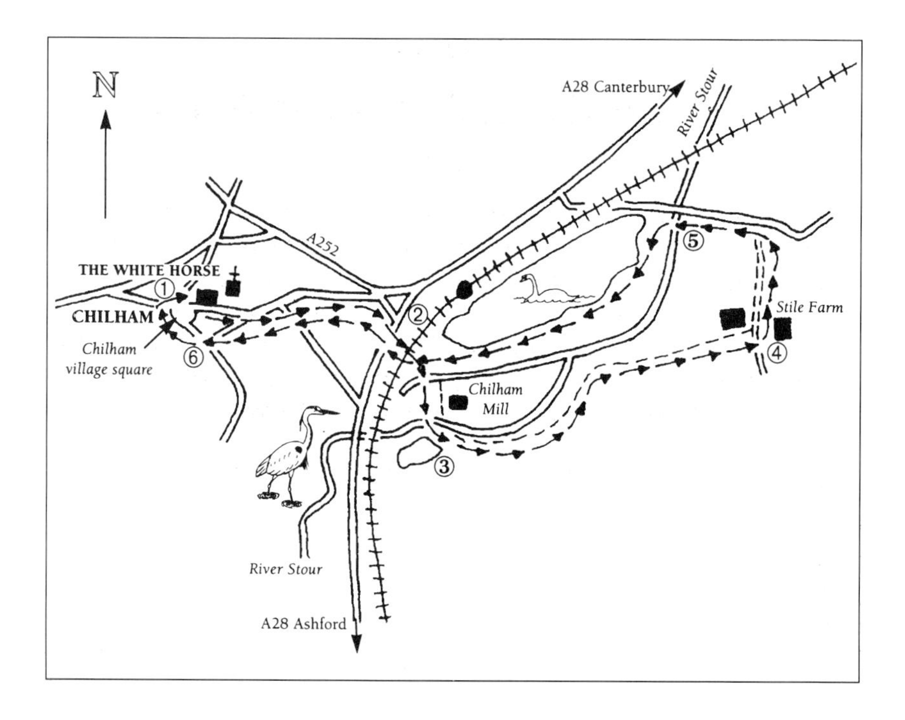

At the end of the path turn right back to the level crossing and retrace your steps, across the A28, along the sliproad, then left along the lane and at the Woolpack continue straight ahead along the lower lane.

6. Turn right uphill at Mountain Street to return to Chilham Square from a different approach.

Notice the old brick Victorian School on the right and the walls of Chilham Castle on the left. The oldest heronry in the country is in the grounds of Chilham Castle. This is a perfect habitat for them as they roost in trees but need open water, such as the lakes, for feeding.

Places of Interest Nearby

Historic *Canterbury*, with its superb cathedral, is only 5 miles north-east of Chilham. (Tourist Information Centre, telephone: 01227 7665677.) If you would like to walk further, the *Stour Valley Walk* continues along the lower ground near the riverside into Canterbury or south or the *North Downs Way* leads across the downs above.

WALK 11

DUNGENESS: A BEACH WALK

Visiting Dungeness is like stepping into another world - vast expanses of shingle, huge wide skies and endless sea, wooden fishing boats pulled up on shingle ridges, red sailed vessels out at sea. Behind the ridge are tiny wooden cottages and huts, dark brown or white with gaily painted windows. The power station is behind. The route follows a footpath south from the Pilot pub, past the lighthouses to the shore and returns the same way.

Fishing boat on the shingle at Dungeness

The sea has formed the strange landscape of Dungeness, its fierce wave action depositing this broad shingle spit - the largest in Europe and it continues to grow. It has dominated the lives of local people. The shifting shingle and often stormy seas have always been treacherous for shipping. The fishermen, who work the seas for the rich harvest of mackerel and herring, also man the lifeboat, which has made many a daring rescue.

Dungeness is also special for plants and animals, designated as a

National Nature Reserve. At first glance the shingle looks barren and dull but many unusual plants have colonised this bleak mass of pebbles and in May and June it is a mass of colour. Water is always a problem in these salty, windswept conditions so the plants have evolved ways to conserve moisture. There are dwarf varieties, such as broom or hebe, low growing with tiny leaves. Others have spiny or thick leathery leaves like the sea holly or prickly bugloss. Rooting in the shingle is hard and these plants are easily damaged so please tread carefully and do not wander across undisturbed shingle. Please also respect the privacy of the people who live and work at Dungeness. Do treat Dungeness sensitively and help to conserve this unique area.

The Pilot, named after the pilots who guided the larger ships safely to shore in these treacherous waters, is a simple workaday building on the outside, single storied, like most buildings at Dungeness. Inside, the welcome is warm and the fish and chips memorable. A pleasant covered verandah has good views out to sea.

Note the 'backstays' hanging on the pub wall, wooden planks with leather straps, used by locals for walking effectively on the shingle - something that has always been hard work! Before the road was built, horse-drawn carts needed special broad wooden wheels to deliver goods along the shingle.

Four types of fish, predictably the Pilot's speciality, are on offer - cod, hake, plaice and skate - but steaks, sandwiches, ploughman's, salads and a range of sweets are also served. A huge selection of alcoholic coffees is available which will certainly warm you up after a bracing winter walk along the shore! Children are welcome to eat here and there is a garden and a special children's menu. No dogs are allowed, however. Beamish, Courage and Theakston bitters, Kronenbourg and Foster's lagers and Strongbow cider are on draught. They also sell their own label wine. Opening hours are from 11 am to 3 pm every day and from 6 pm to 11 pm on Monday to Saturday (closed on Sunday evening). Food is served from 12 noon to 2.30 pm and 6 pm to 9 pm on Monday to Saturday and from 12 noon to 2 pm on Sunday.

Telephone: 01797 320314.

- **HOW TO GET THERE:** From Lydd take the minor road signed to Dungeness, past lakes and marsh. Continue on this road to the coast and the Pilot is on the right on the shingle.
- **PARKING:** There is a large pub car park for patrons. Alternatively, park beside the lighthouse.

- **LENGTH OF THE WALK:** 2½ miles, to the lighthouses and back. Maps: OS Landranger 189 or Explorer 125 (GR 092186).

THE WALK

1. From the Pilot, turn right and walk across the shingle towards the Royal National Lifeboat Institute building. Bear right gradually to join the road near a cottage with a black rectangular tank in front.

This is a tanning copper used for dying and preserving fishing nets and aprons with a dark resin called kutch.

2. Turn left and continue alongside the road, past the lifeboat station, towards the lighthouses and the power station.

To the right are small wooden houses, some with elaborate gardens built from the flotsam and jetsam washed up by the tides. The most famous is the garden of the film director, the late Derek Jarman, with wood, wire and stone arranged to create imaginative sculptures.

3. In front of the first lighthouse the road bears round to the right. (Detour right along the road to visit the old lighthouse or the miniature steam railway.) Continue straight ahead on the footpath, passing the modern lighthouse.

There has been a lighthouse of sorts at Dungeness since 1615 to warn shipping of the hazardous shingle. The sea has steadily receded, making each in turn too far inland – the lighthouse built in 1776 was 500 ft inland one hundred years later! The Victorian lighthouse was replaced by the present one in 1961, in a new position, as the nuclear power plant had impeded the light.

4. Keep going across the shingle down towards the shore. If you wish you can continue further on the footpath which turns right and carries on in front of the power station. After exploring the shore retrace your steps back to the Pilot.

This is an ideal site for a power station, where the sea can be used as cooling water. The endless power lines stretch across the horizon, taking the generated electricity to houses and factories far afield.

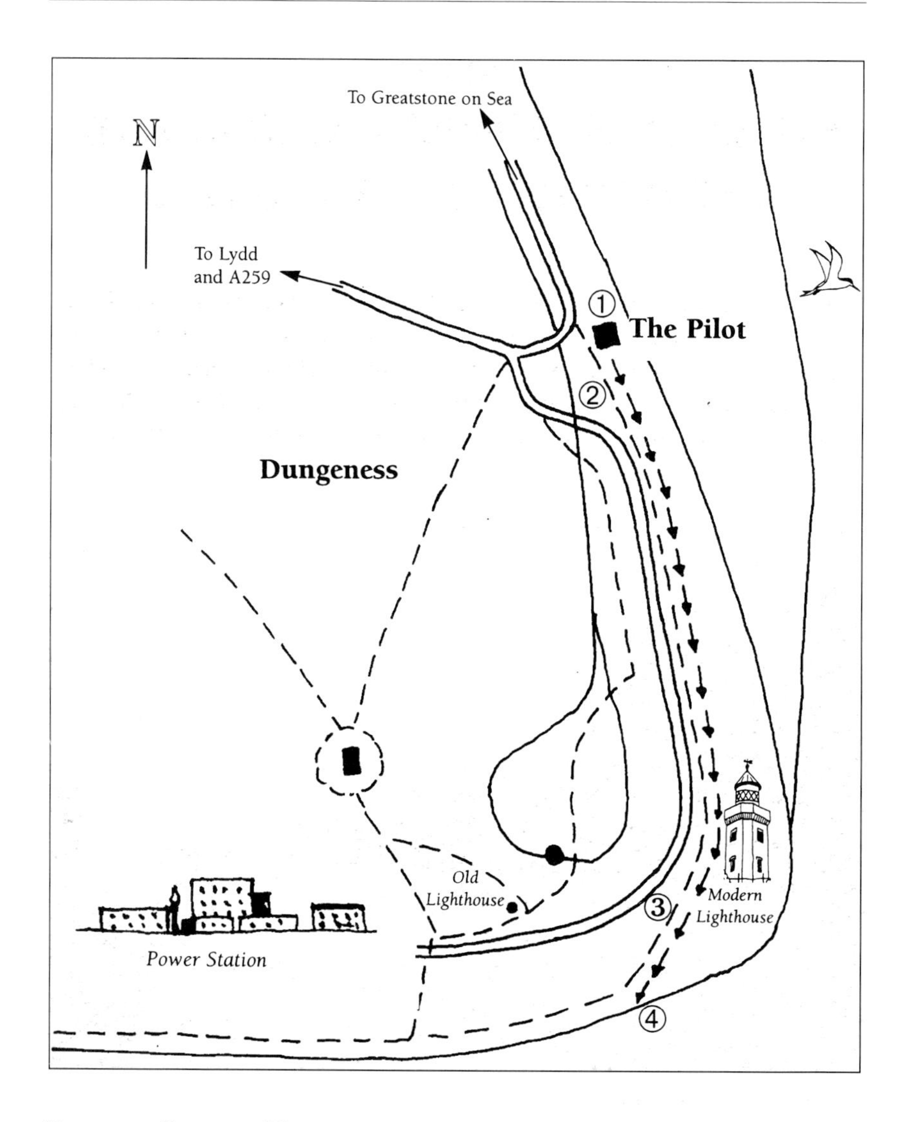

Places of Interest Nearby

The *Romney, Hythe and Dymchurch Railway* is the world's smallest steam and diesel railway. You can take a ride from the station in front of the power station (telephone: 01797 362353). *Dungeness Nuclear Power Station* has a visitor centre with displays explaining the workings of the power station (telephone: 01797 321815).

WALK 12

BURMARSH: ROMNEY MARSH AND THE ROYAL MILITARY CANAL

This walk begins in the sleepy village of Burmarsh in the heart of Romney Marsh, and takes you across the sheep-grazed marsh with its flat open fields separated by reed-filled ditches. Then there is contrast, walking along the tree-lined Royal Military Canal with Roman remains and Norman Lympne Castle on the old seacliffs above.

The Royal Military Canal

Romney Marsh has its own unique atmosphere. The flatness and lack of hedgerows gives a wide, windswept feel and the huge, everchanging skies dwarf everything below. Like so many parts of Kent the coastline has changed dramatically since the Roman Conquest and the River Limen once entered the sea at the foot of the Lympne hills. The estuary of the Limen in the north and the Rother in the south gradually silted up and, as the sea receded, small marshy islands gradually formed. The marshy land was 'inned' or drained in the Middle Ages, bit by bit, to make fertile pasture to fatten sheep and cattle. Palisades of logs and clay were built to hold back the water and drainage ditches dug. Much of the marsh area, including Burmarsh, was in the ownership of the Church and inned by monks. As each new area was drained a church was built in thanksgiving and that is why there are so many on Romney, their spires and towers distinctive landmarks in this flat landscape.

The Royal Military Canal, stretching from Rye to Hythe, follows the route of the ancient shoreline from which the sea has retreated. It was built as a defence against Napoleon as it was thought the marshes were the most likely landing point for the French armies massed at Boulogne as they were easy to land on and difficult to defend.

The name of the Shepherd and Crook pub in Burmarsh reflects the importance of sheep grazing in the local economy. The world famous Romney sheep, large-headed with their long Roman faces and long, rich fleeces, were bred on these fertile marshes. This is an attractive cream building beside the ancient church and it offers friendly, helpful service and a relaxed, cosy feel. The saloon bar is particularly welcoming, laden with copper and brasses and with a blazing fire in cold weather. A freehouse renowned for its high quality real ales, Adnams, Benskins and Greene King IPA are usually available plus guest beers, Stella and Heineken lagers and Blackthorn cider. There is a good range of inexpensive pub food, including home-made turkey, ham and mushroom pie and chips, steak and kidney pie, fish and chips, ploughman's, jacket potatoes and sandwiches. The opening times are from 11.30 am to 3 pm and 7 pm to 11 pm on Monday to Saturday and 12 noon to 3 pm and 7 pm to 10.30 pm on Sunday. Food is served from 12 noon to 2 pm and 7.30 pm to 9 pm daily except for Sunday and Monday evenings.

Telephone: 01303 872336.

- **HOW TO GET THERE:** From Dymchurch, travelling on the A259 towards Hythe, take Burmarsh Road on the left on the outskirts of Dymchurch. Follow the road for approx 1½ miles into the village. The pub is beside the church.
- **PARKING:** There is roadside parking in the village centre or along Shear Way.
- **LENGTH OF THE WALK:** 5 miles. Maps: OS Landranger 189 or Explorer 138 (GR 102320).

The Walk

1. From the main entrance of the pub turn left along Shear Way and continue along the lane. Pass a cottage on the right and before Abbots Farmhouse turn left, following the footpath signs, across a small paddock, over a stile and across a ditch, then right along the edge of the ditch. Continue straight ahead and pass farm buildings on the right.

The ditches are full of plants in the spring and summer. Some of the more distinctive are water plantain with delicate pink flowers, bur reed with its round, spikey flowerheads and yellow flag iris. Dragonflies and damselflies flit above and glistening whirligig beetles spin in groups on the water surface. You may hear the marsh frogs plopping into dykes and in the breeding season their raucous croak is hard to miss.

Beyond the buildings cross a ditch and continue on the opposite side towards cliffs. Cross another ditch and continue straight ahead.

2. Turn left onto the road and soon after turn right along a lane signed to a caravan and camping site. At the end of the lane cross the bridge over the Royal Military Canal.

3. Turn right along the footpath that winds through the woodland edging the canal (take the upper footpath rather than the broader bridlepath that is further from the canal).

You can just glimpse the canal through the trees on the right. It was refortified during the Second World War and you will pass a concrete pill box on your left, built to conceal and protect guns, one of many alongside the canal. The high fence on the left edges Port Lympne Zoo and signs warn that antelope and bison are grazing nearby!

Ignore the Saxon Shore Way path uphill to the left. At the second path detour left for good views of the castles.

The ruins of the Roman castle are halfway down, built to protect the harbour which once lay below. Higher up and to the east is Norman Lympne Castle, on the site of the original Roman watchtower, and St Stephen's church alongside that dates from the same era.

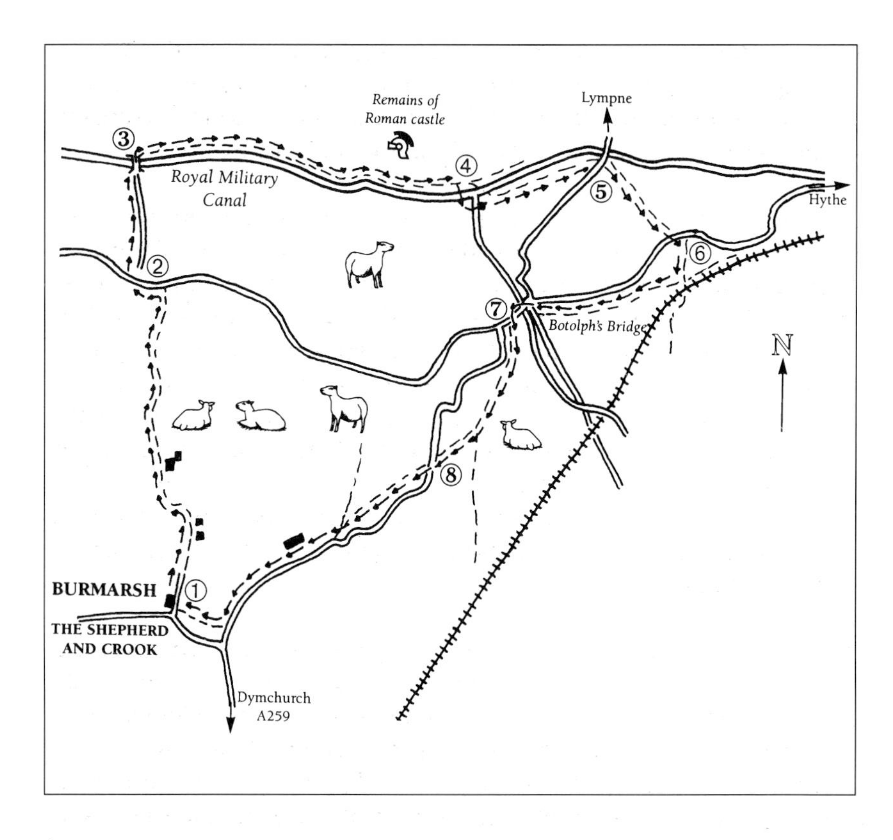

4. Turn right and cross the canal on the footbridge by West Hythe sluices, then go left and continue along the other bank.

The canal is important nowadays for controlling water levels on the marshes, acting as a reservoir of water in the summer, and water is pumped into it to drain marshes and prevent flooding in winter.

5. At a road with a curved brick bridge, cross the road and leave the canal, taking the footpath between industrial buildings and houses. Walk diagonally to the left across the field to the far left corner to the left of a big row of poplars. Cross the stile and plank over the dyke, then turn left and follow the field edge to the left. Cross the stile in the far corner onto the road. Cross the road and climb another stile into the opposite field. Follow the left hand fenceline and ditch across the field back onto open marsh.

6. At a ditch junction, ignore the footbridge and paths to the left and turn right through a gate (very rickety gate and stile). Walk straight ahead to the hedgerow, then bear left and walk alongside the hedgerow, parallel with the road. Climb the stile at Botolph's Bridge onto the road.

7. Cross the road and in front of Botolph's Bridge Inn turn right and immediately left along the road that runs along the side of the pub. Then take the footpath left, just before some industrial buildings (also marked 'Romney Marsh circular walks'). Cross in front of a little cottage and walk diagonally to the left across the field to a yellow topped waymarker post to the left of a telegraph post by a tree-lined ditch. Cross the dried-up ditch and continue straight ahead across the next field to the yellow post beside the stile in the opposite fenceline. Continue straight ahead across the next field to the marker post at the corner of the fence ahead. Cross the ditch on a low bridge and bear diagonally right across the arable field (ignore the marker indicating along the fenceline).

8. At the road turn left and then right soon after onto another path across a field (if too overgrown or unclear, keep following the road). The path leads across fields, finally emerging in a small paddock. Cross the stile onto the road and turn right, passing Great Lathe Farm. Continue on the road until nearing the road junction. Turn onto a path to the right that leads straight across an arable field and then alongside the back of houses. Take the narrow path between the houses that leads back to the pub.

Places of Interest Nearby

Great Lathe Farm has a farming museum, children's facilities and a brilliant tea shop (not open in winter) (telephone: 01303 873618). The village of *Lympne*, set on the hillside above the canal, is worth exploring with its Roman ruins and Norman church and castle (Lympne Castle, telephone: 01303 267571). *Port Lympne Zoo* has magnificent grounds where the animals are kept in large natural enclosures (telephone: 01303 264646).

WALK 13

WHITSTABLE: SEAWALLS AND OYSTERS

Whitstable has its own special maritime flavour - the salty tang of sea air, long shingle beaches broken by wave-lashed breakwaters, masts of boats, old wooden warehouses and a still thriving harbour. The walk leads from the former boatbuilding areas, along old seawalls and through the harbour, then up onto Tankerton Slopes for bracing walking and wide sea views.

Whitstable harbour

The sea has always been the key to Whitstable's prosperity. The town grew in importance as the port for Canterbury from the 17th century. By the 19th century it was exporting thousands of tons of hops and corn and importing coal. A worldwide diving industry also developed, built on the existing salvage skills of local fishermen. Oysters, however, have always been the most renowned product of the town.

The sea has also taken its toll on the town, constantly battering away at the coastline so that it is now far inland from its position in Roman times. In 1583 the first seawall was built, running seaward of the present harbour, but it was often breached and an inner seawall was built in 1780. The sea continued to encroach despite constant battles and there were several serious floods. During the 1950s the first concrete seawall was built. The battle against the force of the sea continues today but current sea defences concentrate on raising the beach to force waves to break before they reach the wall.

The white weatherboarded Old Neptune pub lies in a very exposed position, high on the shingle beach with superb views out to sea. It was severely damaged in a flood in 1853 and its successor reduced to a few planks in 1897. It was rebuilt using materials from the ruined cottages in 1912 and again after damage in the floods of 1938 and 1953.

This friendly and characterful pub serves an excellent range of food. There is always a wide choice of specials on the board incorporating fresh fish bought at the harbour. More basic pub fare available includes sandwiches, snacks and children's meals. Children are welcome and there are plenty of tables outside alongside the shingle beach. The Old Neptune is a freehouse offering a good range of real ales such as Flowers Original, Fuller's London Pride and Greene King Abbot Ale. Draught Strongbow and Scrumpy Jack ciders and Stella and Heineken lagers are also served. The pub is open all day, seven days a week - 11 am to 11 pm on Monday to Saturday and 12 noon to 10.30 pm on Sunday. Food is served from midday to 7.30 pm every day.

Telephone: 01227 272262.

- **HOW TO GET THERE:** Take the A290 towards Whitstable and bear left under the railway bridge on the B2205. Continue along High Street and, if requiring parking, follow the one way system to Harbour Street. On foot from the car park turn left and walk into the centre along Harbour Street. At the junction with High Street turn right up Terry's Lane and left again along Island Wall. The Old Neptune is on the foreshore on the right through Neptune Gap. Alternatively, you could start the walk at point 6, close to Keams Yard car park.
- **PARKING:** Use the large free car park opposite the harbour (see above) or Keams Yard car park on the right where Terry's Lane crosses Island Wall.
- **LENGTH OF THE WALK:** 2½ miles. Maps: OS Landranger 179 or Explorer 150 (GR 105666).

The Walk

1. Turn left out of the pub and walk along the seawall.

Look for the 'Favourite', an old sailing yawl once used for dredging the oyster beds. Several of the largest boatyards were situated just behind the seawall. The last commercial craft made here was a pilot boat launched in 1983 but leisure craft are still made and repaired in the town.

2. At Horsebridge continue along the front past the Royal Native Oyster Stores.

The slipway at The Horsebridge was once used by horse-drawn carts unloading cargo from the flat bottomed sailing craft that could sit on the seabed at low tide. They were used until the harbour opened in 1832. In 1898 the large Royal Native Oyster Stores were built with two large holding tanks beneath the floor which held the daily catch until it was despatched by rail to London. It is now a seafood restaurant serving Whitstable oysters and other fish dishes.

Continue along the shingle beach if the tide allows or along the seawall to Reeves Beach.

This is named after William Reeves, foreman of the Company of Oyster Fishers, who developed his family business of block and mast making here. The tarred weatherboarded stores, workshops and cottages clustered above the shingle beach retain the feel of that era.

From Reeves Beach continue along the shingle to the harbour. Explore the harbour area on East Quay and continue past the fish warehouses along the quayside to the road.

3. Turn left and walk along the road for a short distance past a garage, swimming pool and bowling alley. Turn left onto Beach Walk and follow this round to the promenade along the bottom of Tankerton Slopes. Walk along the seafront as far as you wish.

Tankerton developed as a seaside resort in the 1890s until transport improved to allow visitors to travel further afield. It still retains a genteel Victorian seaside resort air. Look for 'The Street', a long shingle

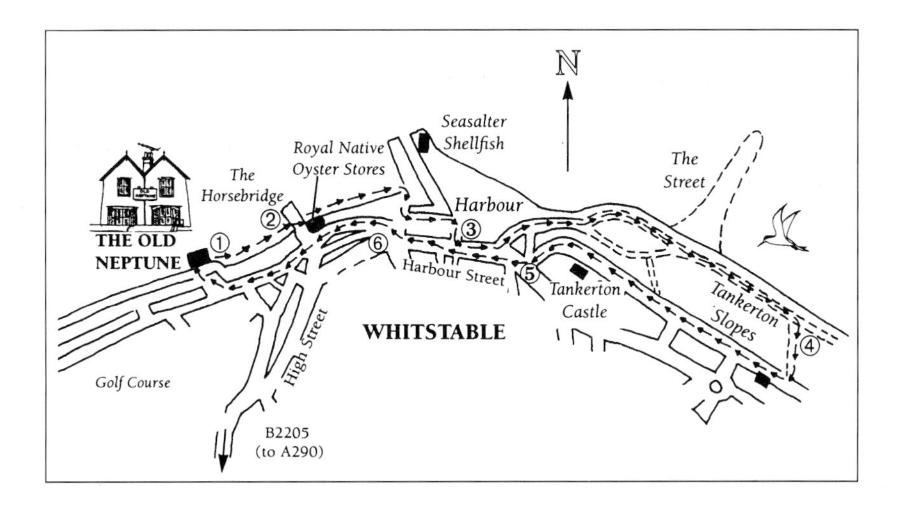

spit stretching out to sea that can be walked at low tide. High tide creates unusual wave patterns across it.

4. There is a series of stepped paths along the promenade that lead up Tankerton Slopes. When you wish, turn right and climb steps up the slopes and then go right again to walk along the top of the slopes and then continue downhill along Tower Hill Road.

You may wish to detour left into the grounds of Tankerton Castle, built in 1790 as the country retreat for a millionaire London merchant but now a public park.

5. Turn right at the bottom of the hill and continue back into town along Harbour Street.

6. Just past the harbour entrance bear right along Seawall back to Horsebridge. Cross Horsebridge and walk back along Island Wall to the Old Neptune.

Places of Interest Nearby

The fascinating *Oyster Fishery Exhibition* is on East Quay (telephone: 01227 272003) and in Oxford Street there is the *Whitstable Museum* which explores the area's maritime history (telephone: 01227 276998).

WALK 14

WESTBERE AND FORDWICH: RIVER, LAKES AND MARSHES

This short and easy walk takes you from the sleepy village of Westbere and, following the course of the Great Stour upstream, across the windswept and quiet Westbere Marshes and lakes to the historic small town of Fordwich, once a bustling port.

The Stour at Fordwich

In medieval times the Stour was navigable to large craft when it was linked to the sea by the wide Wantsum Channel, so both Westbere and Fordwich have a rich maritime history.

The attractive lakes to the south of Westbere, edged with reeds and overhanging willow, are the flooded holes left after the excavation of sand and gravel. The reedbeds and wet grassland surrounding the lakes provide homes for many waterbirds and other wetland creatures and in the winter large numbers of ducks and swans gather here. Wildlife and man seem to live side by side on these lakes – anglers line the edges, patiently waiting for a bite, and dinghy sailors silently tack across the waters while the birds continue to dabble and dive nearby.

In the village of Westbere itself is the delightful half-timbered Yew Tree - built in 1306 and an inn since the 15th century. Outside there is a pleasant garden overlooking the lakes.

The cosy atmosphere and hearty food has made the inn popular with locals and visitors alike. Opening hours are from 11 am to 3 pm and 6.30 pm to 11 pm on Monday to Saturday and from 12 noon to 4 pm and 7 pm to 10.30 pm on Sunday. Food is served each day during opening hours and comprises hearty snacks and traditional pub fare such as sausage and crusty bread or steak and kidney pie. Specials include winter roasts, vegetarian dishes such as stuffed peppers and starters such as pork, Stilton and celery soup. In the evenings there is a wider à la carte menu. A separate pudding menu offers a wide choice from substantial fruit pies and sponge pudding to icecreams. The pub stocks Shepherd Neame and Bass real ales, Scrumpy Jack cider, Hürlimann and Carling lagers and a good range of French and Australian wines.

Telephone: 01227 710501.

- **HOW TO GET THERE:** Approaching from Canterbury, take the A28, signed for Sturry and Margate. Pass through Sturry and turn right immediately beyond the village, signed 'Westbere'. Follow the lane into the village and the Yew Tree is on the right.
- **HOW TO GET THERE:** There is a small pub car park (busy at weekends) where you may leave your car in the mornings, with the permission of the landlord, provided that you will use the pub later. There is also a certain amont of roadside parking in the village.
- **HOW TO GET THERE:** 3 miles. Maps: OS Landranger 179 or Explorer 150 (GR 194611).

THE WALK

1. From the Yew Tree turn right along the lane and continue straight ahead past modern housing where the lane bears left.

2. At the end of the road turn right and cross over the railway. Continue straight ahead on a footpath which leads beside a large lake.

3. At a footpath junction turn right and walk with the lake on the right and River Great Stour on the left, draining the wet grassland via several reed-edged ditches.

You may see large brown cormorants sitting in the trees at the edge of the water or spreading their wings out to dry. If you are lucky you can watch the ungainly flight of the massive swans with their heavy wingbeats and noisy watery landings.

Continue on this meandering path, passing pockets of willow carr woodland on the right and more lakes beyond the Stour on the left, until you reach the road.

Tolls were levied to cross Fordwich bridge and until recently it was the duty of the landlord of the George and Dragon to collect the tolls.

4. Turn left and cross over the bridge to detour into Fordwich. Alternatively, to continue the walk, turn right and walk along the road for a short distance.

It's hard to imagine that the quiet little town of Fordwich was once a busy medieval and Tudor port. Owned largely by the powerful Abbot of St Augstine's Abbey in Canterbury from the 11th century, it was an obvious landing point for materials needed for the abbey. It flourished as the port for Canterbury and even the stone for Canterbury Cathedral was brought from Normandy via Fordwich. The tolls collected on goods landed at the large wharves that lined the river banks and the employment generated brought wealth and prosperity. It was made a 'Borough' in Norman times but it gradually declined as the Wantsum silted up. It retains its earlier designation and now lays claim to the title of 'the smallest town in England'. There are plenty of reminders of its former importance – look for the half-timbered Town Hall and gaol, the 15th-century church with its slender shingled spire and Monk's Hall cottages, based on a medieval house.

Opposite Fordwich Garage turn right onto a path that meanders through willow carr.

5. Where the path meets the drive to the recreation ground turn left onto a track alongside football pitches and turn right in front of the small pavilion to walk along the hedgerow towards the miniature railway. Cross through the gap in the hedge and continue walking alongside the railway line (full size!).

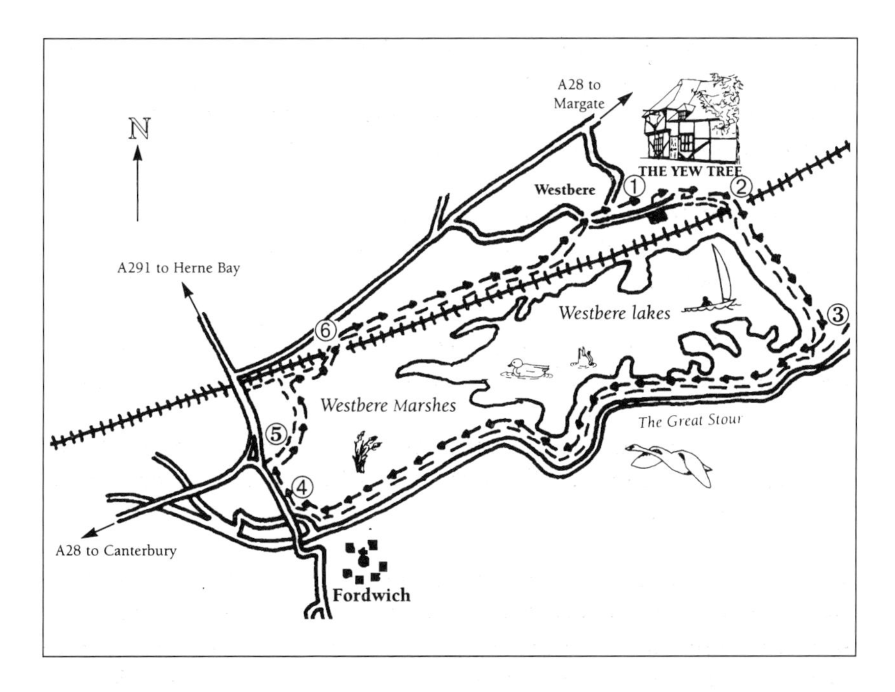

6. Cross over the railway line at the pedestrian crossing and turn right along the path that runs parallel with the line for just over ½ mile. Follow the same path as it bears left across the field away from the railway to the road. Turn right and walk along the road through Westbere, back to the Yew Tree.

Downstream from the port of Fordwich, near the Stour's junction with the Wantsum Channel, Westbere was ideally situated for smugglers and pirates, keen to avoid the duty levied at the port.

PLACES OF INTEREST NEARBY

Stodmarsh National Nature Reserve, to the east along the Stour, is made up of large areas of reedbed, wet meadows and open water and attracts large numbers of wetland birds. There are hides and a trail (telephone: 01233 812525). Historic *Canterbury*, with its superb cathedral and host of other attractions, is only 2 miles west of Fordwich (Tourist Information Centre: 01227 766567).

WALK 15

GROVE FERRY: BETWEEN THE STOURS

Walk out from this once important river crossing point, where a ferry took passengers across the formerly wide channel for centuries until 1964, then continue along the Little Stour, across fields with the remains of ancient salt workings and back along the meandering Great Stour. This is an extremely quiet area with a remote, open feel and wide views.

The Stour at Grove Ferry

The landscape is very different nowadays from a thousand years ago when most of the flat land that you walk over would have been under water. The Wantsum Channel ran across these fields, separating Thanet from the mainland and providing a shipping channel between the Thames and Sandwich and, hence, the Continent. The channel gradually silted up leaving large areas of marsh that regularly flooded. The marshes were gradually drained in the 16th and 17th centuries by

Flemish refugees so that the fertile soil could be used for grazing. The land has been further drained and is now used for arable crops and orchards as well. The Little Stour, dug as a drainage channel in 1562 from Wickhambreaux to Plucks Gutter, was one of the final attempts to keep the Wantsum navigable.

The Grove Ferry Inn, beside the Great Stour, dates from the 17th century and was rebuilt in 1831 as a coaching inn, an important staging post on the road between Herne Bay and Dover. The pub has long links with the ferry, which was, until recently, the only way of crossing the river. Smuggling was rife in east Kent in the 17th and 18th centuries and one ferryman was in league with smuggling gangs. If excisemen were pursuing the smugglers he would lock the ferry and go to bed so they couldn't cross to give chase and contraband was often lowered into the river to avoid detection.

This large, friendly pub, with a spacious beer garden and shady willow trees beside the river, is ideal for families. There is a riverside restaurant and the pub also owns a licensed boat, the MV *Grove Ferry*, which takes regular trips along the river during the summer months. Opening hours are from 11 am to 3 pm and 6 pm to 11 pm on Monday to Saturday and from 12 noon to 10.30 pm on Sunday. Food is served at lunchtime from 12 noon to 2.30 pm and in the evening from 7 pm to 10 pm (9.30 pm on Sunday).

The pub's range of bar food includes filled baguettes, jacket potatoes, burgers and ploughman's and more substantial meals such as steaks, pastas and chilli. There are always chalkboard specials too, and a Sunday selection of roasts. The evening menu is more extensive and there is a good wine list. Children can choose from their own menu or opt for a reduced size adult meal. Courage, John Smith's and Theakston are among the draught beers, alongside Hofmeister, Kronenbourg and Foster's lagers and Guinness. Dogs are welcome in the bar area.

Telephone: 01227 860302.

- **HOW TO GET THERE:** Approaching from Canterbury, take the A28, signed for Sturry and Margate. Pass through Sturry and continue to Upstreet. Turn right just after the village, signed to Grove Ferry. The road crosses the railway and then the river and the pub is on the left hand side beside the river.
- **PARKING** There is a car park for pub customers (ask the landlord before leaving your car there while you walk as it gets very busy at summer lunchtimes and weekends). The adjacent Grove Ferry picnic

area has a large public car park.

- **LENGTH OF THE WALK:** 4½ miles. Maps: OS Landranger 179 or Explorer 150 (GR 236633).

THE WALK

1. From the Grove Ferry Inn turn left and walk through the entrance to Grove Ferry picnic area. Go left onto the riverside path and turn right and walk along the river bank. As you approach a small marina, towards the end of the picnic area, cross the grass to the right and climb a stile leading onto the road.

This picnic area is on the site of Canterbury lavender fields and the tall chimney near the inn was part of the lavender distillery. It is now a popular spot for riverside relaxing. There are lots of moored boats and many anglers - I watched two boys proudly photographing the huge pike they had just caught.

2. After a few yards turn left into a field and take a footpath to the right, signed 'Saxon Shore Way' and 'Stour Valley Walk'. Follow the well marked path across fields to the Little Stour.

3. Cross on the footbridge and turn left to walk alongside the Little Stour along the Saxon Shore Way.

Straight ahead the church spire of West Stourmouth stands out. This tiny church dates from before the Norman Conquest but is no longer used. Centuries ago the River Stour would have emptied into the Wantsum Channel near here and the village would have been important for shipping.

Follow the path past a pumping station to a small footbridge just before an orchard sheltered by tall poplars begins.

4. Leave the Saxon Shore Way, cross the footbridge and walk across the field along a fragmented hedgerow to meet the Great Stour again.

Ahead is the distinctive silhouette of Sarre Mill and in the distance flat, wide views towards Thanet. The flat fields are drained by a series of ditches, often reed-filled.

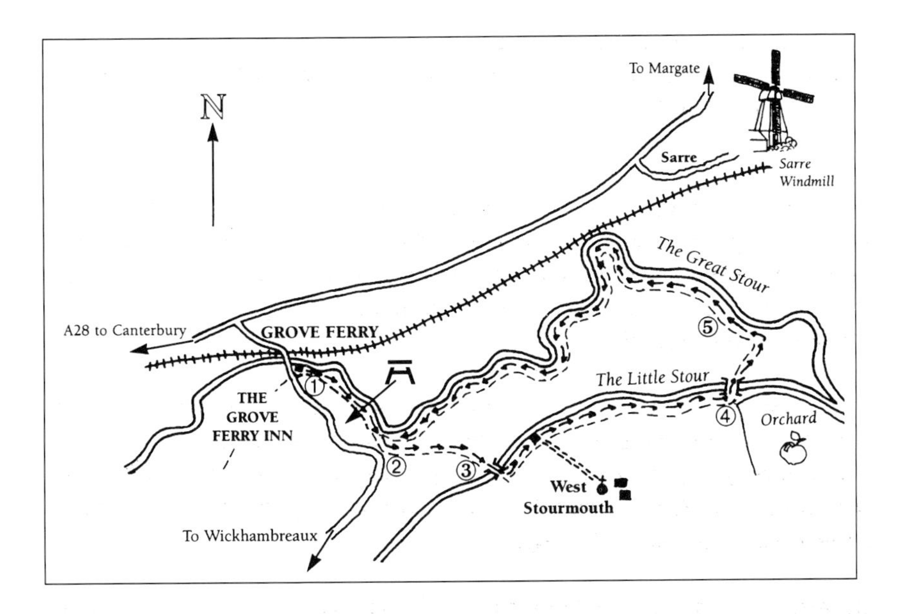

5. Turn left and walk along the field edge beside the river all the way back to Grove Ferry.

Salt was a valuable commodity in earlier times as the main method of food preservation. The marshland would have been regularly flooded by sea water and in these fields alongside the river are the remains of old salt works. One method of salt collection was to soak bunches of hazel faggots in the briney seawater, and then boil them to evaporate off the water, leaving a coating of salt on the faggots.

Places of Interest Nearby

Stodmarsh National Nature Reserve (telephone: 01233 812525) lies to the south. *Sarre Mill* (telephone: 01843 847573), an old smock mill now restored to full working order, can be visited in the summer months and is just north-east of Grove Ferry, up the A28.

WALK 16

ST NICHOLAS AT WADE: WANTSUM WANDERINGS

A peaceful stroll from this historic village, across Wade Marsh, to the sea. Then bracing walking along the seawalls to follow the River Wantsum back inland. The route is a must for naturalists, with interesting flowers in the spring and summer and large numbers of waders and wildfowl overwintering on the marsh and coast. This circuit, across flat terrain, is one of the Wantsum Walks and is clearly waymarked throughout.

Looking out to sea

The countryside around St Nicholas at Wade looks very different now from when the Wantsum Channel flowed through it eight hundred years ago and it was a thriving maritime settlement. The village developed around one of the few crossing points to Thanet, a ford shallow enough to wade across at one time, hence the 'wade' in its name. Its 12th-century parish church is named after St Nicholas, the patron saint of seafarers, which further reflects its maritime links. The village continued to prosper even after the Wantsum had shrunk to a stream as it became an important stop on the coaching route between Canterbury and Ramsgate in the 17th century. Both the old hostelries were brake houses for the coaches and there was even a third inn at one time.

The historic Bell, in the centre of the village, was originally built in 1500 as a farm. It became a pub in the 17th century and thrived as a coaching inn. In 1622 the landlord was censored by the ecclesiastical authorities for failing to close during evening prayers as too many villagers were drinking instead of attending church! Like so many parts of Kent, the village had smuggling links and there are bricked up tunnels beneath the inn that reputedly linked with the Wantsum Channel.

The pub has a wonderful atmosphere, with wood panels, beams and an open fire in the cosy bar in winter where chestnuts can be roasted. Local seafood is a speciality here and up to seven varieties of fish are on offer, such as shell-on prawns, lobster, red sea bream and grilled sardines. There are also plenty of meat dishes including steaks and ham, and home-cooked vegetarian meals are available on request. The menu changes regularly and is seasonal, offering turkey, roast goose and heartier meals in winter and more salads, fresh crab and such like in summer. There is also a good range of bar snacks. Puddings are excellent too - both the hot substantial ones in the winter, sponge puddings, crepes suzette and crumbles, and the lighter summer choices. This freehouse offers four regular real ales, Flowers IPA, Wadworth 6X, Boddingtons and Bass and a guest beer. Draught Guinness, Blackthorn cider and Carlsberg, Heineken and Stella lagers are also served. Children are welcome in the dining area, the games room and the attractive garden and there is a special children's menu.

Telephone: 01843 847250.

- **HOW TO GET THERE:** St Nicholas at Wade is just off the A299, Thanet Way, west of Margate. From the A28/A299 roundabout take the minor road signed to St Nicholas at Wade. Turn left over Thanet Way into the village. At the junction with The Street continue straight ahead past the church. The Bell is on the right.
- **PARKING:** Walking customers can use the pub car park and there is some roadside parking in the village.
- **LENGTH OF THE WALK:** 5½ miles. Maps: OS Landranger 179 or Explorer 150 (GR 266666).

The Walk

1. From the Bell turn left and walk along The Street towards the church.

The village of St Nicholas at Wade has some fine houses, most dating from the 16th and 17th centuries. The stepped and curving gables are Dutch in style, influenced by European settlers fleeing from religious persecution in Europe in Tudor times. The tower of St Nicholas' church can be seen from miles around, and was an important landmark for shipping.

Turn right along Shuart Lane and continue to Shuart Farm buildings.

Wade Marsh stretches out ahead to the sea and the twin towers of Reculver church are visible to the left - a distinctive landmark throughout this walk.

Shuart Farm was once a much bigger settlement. There was a large church here but it was abandoned and all trace of it above ground had gone by the end of the 17th century. Perhaps the population was decimated by the Black Death or the livelihoods of many people were lost after the Wantsum silted up.

2. Bear left along the footpath in front of Shuart Farm (ignore a bridleway to the right). The leafy lane leads out to grazing marsh and arable land alongside drainage ditches and onto the old seawall. Follow the well marked path along the seawall towards the railway line that runs parallel with the sea.

You are now walking along the raised earthen seawall above fields separated by a network of reed-fringed dykes, which serve both to drain the land and act as field boundaries. Most of the dykes, or sewers as they are known, were created in the 12th and 13th centuries when marshy land around the Wantsum was drained or 'inned' by monks from Canterbury. Until recently all these marshes were pasture and were used for sheep but much has now been further drained and is used for arable farming as the silty soils are so fertile. In winter you may see flocks of lapwings and large numbers of Brent geese and swans feeding on the marsh.

Cross the railway line and continue along the old seawall towards the

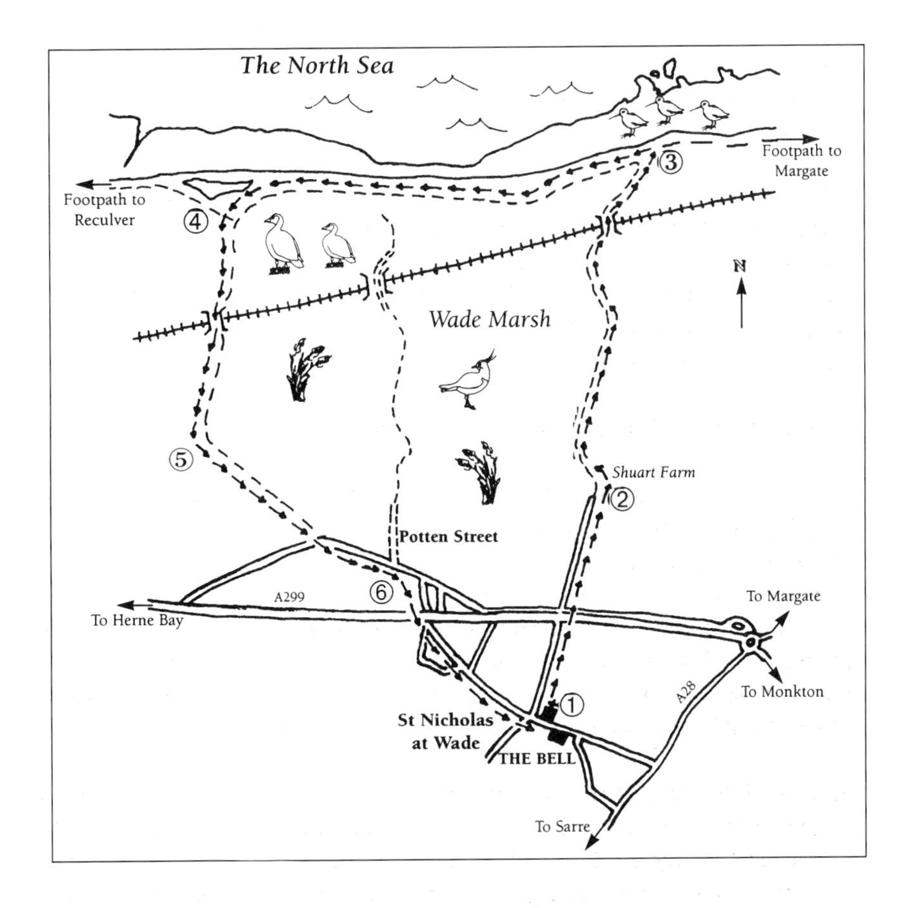

modern concrete wall ahead that now separates us from the sea.

3. Turn left and walk along the concrete 'promenade' towards Reculver.

The modern seawall has been built up to a much higher level than the old Shuart Wall as the sea level is still rising and flooding remains a threat. There are fine views across the flat marshes back to St Nicholas at Wade, west to Reculver or east to Thanet.

Look for a small salt lagoon inside the seawall. The high shingle bank in front of it provides a further sea defence and is used as a high tide roost for shorebirds.

4. Beside the lagoon, turn left by the Coldharbour interpretive board, which gives more information on the wildlife of the area, and walk inland. (You can easily extend this walk by continuing along the seawall to Reculver and looping back to rejoin this route by the railway.)

The broad ditch on your right is the River Wantsum, all that now remains of the ancient Wantsum sea channel. This was once wide enough for large ships but it gradually silted up during the Middle Ages. It flows under the seawall through a sluice to the sea, where the freshwater is welcomed by gulls and waders, who congregate nearby, feeding and bathing in the flow. The original point where medieval ships entered the Wantsum Channel from the Thames, Old Haven, is further west towards Reculver. Around 1486, as the original channel was silting up, the Archbishop of Canterbury had a new, more direct channel cut to the sea, called 'New Haven', and the modern sluice from the Wantsum is named after this channel.

Cross the railway, ignoring the loop of the Wantsum Way leading right towards Reculver, and continue along the path beside Wantsum stream.

5. Bear left onto a track that leads to a farm and turn left along the road in front of the farm.

The tall trees lining the road here are elms. This area is one of the few remaining strongholds of the elm where Dutch Elm disease has not taken its toll. Some are dying at the crown but many others remain healthy and all have thrown up many new shoots or suckers from the base.

Continue along the lane to Potten Street, once one of the ancient ways across the island.

6. Continue straight ahead and then right onto the bridge crossing over Thanet Way. Follow the road back into St Nicholas at Wade.

Places of Interest Nearby

Sarre Mill lies to the south of St Nicholas at Wade, near the centre of Sarre village. This old smock mill is open during the summer and can be seen in full working order (telephone: 01843 847573).

WALK 17

FOLKESTONE: DRAMATIC CLIFFS AND WILD WARREN

This walk begins with bracing clifftop walking on the North Downs Way, accompanied by the salty tang of sea air and wide views out to sea. The route then slowly descends into the Warren and meanders through this fascinating undercliff area before climbing steeply back up the cliffs.

The cliffs at Dover

Folkestone Warren lies just to the east of the town and here you have the chance to wander through a strange, hummocky landscape, the result of landslips caused by the powerful lashing of the sea. This wild, unspoilt area is a marvellous jumble of fern-carpeted woodland, scrub, grassland and towering chalk cliffs. It is now a nature reserve as a wide range of plants grow in this sheltered spot. The trees are mainly sycamore interspersed with ash, hawthorn and cherry; hart's tongue fern and feathery mosses lie below. These in turn provide homes for many creatures and the scrub and tussocky grassland on the woodland edge supply further habitats.

Perched on the clifftop beside the old toll road between Folkestone and Dover, the Valiant Sailor pub at Capel-le-Ferne has been a favourite haunt of travellers and smugglers for centuries. The present building is fairly modern but a pub certainly stood here in the 18th century when the road was a major turnpike route and the toll point was opposite. Adventurous travellers, seeking to avoid paying the high toll on the road, would use clifftop paths instead. One such was Edna, a former landlady, who used to regularly ride her horse and cart along the cliffs. She died when the cart went out of control and plunged over the side. Her ghost is reputed to haunt the pub, knocking over the occasional bottle or glass!

This friendly hostelry is part of the Berni chain and offers their standard menu which includes steaks, chicken and fried fish dishes. In addition there is a regularly changed specials list and lighter snacks and sandwiches are also served. There is a children's menu too. Tea and coffee are available all day. A variety of draught beer is on offer, Boddingtons, Wadworth, Whitbread Best, Heineken, Stella, Guinness and Murphy's. A detailed wine list is available at the bar. Outside you will find a spacious garden with a bouncy castle in the summer. The pub is open from 11 am to 11 pm every day and food is served from 12 noon to 3 pm and 6.30 pm to 10 pm. Dogs are allowed in the garden.

Telephone: 01303 252401.

- **HOW TO GET THERE:** Take the B2011 out of Folkestone, signed 'Capel-le-Ferne'. The Valiant Sailor pub is on the right hand side just after Crete Road East joins the B road from the left.
- **PARKING:** Walkers using the Valiant Sailor may leave their cars in the pub car park. There is also some roadside parking in Capel-le-Ferne.
- **LENGTH OF THE WALK:** 3½ miles. Maps: OS Landranger 179 or Explorer 138 (GR 242378).

THE WALK

NB: The ascent and descent of the cliffs is on clearly marked and stepped paths but it is, nevertheless, quite arduous. For those who prefer an easier walk, a linear walk along the clifftops is a pleasant alternative.

1. From the Valiant Sailor pub turn left and immediately left again onto the footpath leading alongside the pub, past a caravan site and out onto the clifftop. Turn left and walk along the clifftop path, following North

Downs Way markers. Continue along the North Downs Way for about 1¼ miles, passing the Battle of Britain memorial, a clifftop café and more caravans.

The Battle of Britain was fought in the skies above the Channel in 1940. The poignant sculpture of a flak-jacketed young airman looking out across the Channel commemorates the RAF pilots who convincingly defeated the Lutfwaffe, which marked a turning point in the Second World War. Anti-aircraft guns were also positioned along the clifftops and you may notice crumbling, overgrown concrete structures that are all that now remain of the gun emplacements.

2. At the end of the caravan park where a footpath leads up left, take the footpath right, signed 'Folkestone Warren'. The path down is very steep but stepped and zig-zagging.

As you descend there are stunning views out to sea - white cliffs to the left and Folkestone to the right with its harbour and ferries and other craft ploughing in and out. Chalk-loving plants abound in the tussocky grass, giving splashes of colour in season - scented purple marjoram, blue scabious, and carpets of thyme where the grass is shorter. In summer there is a constant hum of insects gathering nectar: bees, hoverflies, and colourful butterflies - blues, marbled whites and browns.

Look back up to the towering chalk cliffs - the different layers of chalk are clearly visible, some mottled with layers of flints, others brilliant white. At one time the area was grazed by rabbits, sheep and cattle which kept the grass short and prevented shrubs from growing. Since grazing ceased the shrubs have taken over in many places - dogwood, distinctive with its red bark, wayfaring tree with its white flowers and red berries, purple flowering buddleia that is so attractive to butterflies, and wild clematis that climbs over the other shrubs and whose clusters of feathery seeds in the autumn give its common name 'old man's beard'.

At the bottom bear right and continue alongside the railway line.

3. Ignore the footpath to the left over the railway unless you want to detour down to the beach. Bear right at the first post, following the main path.

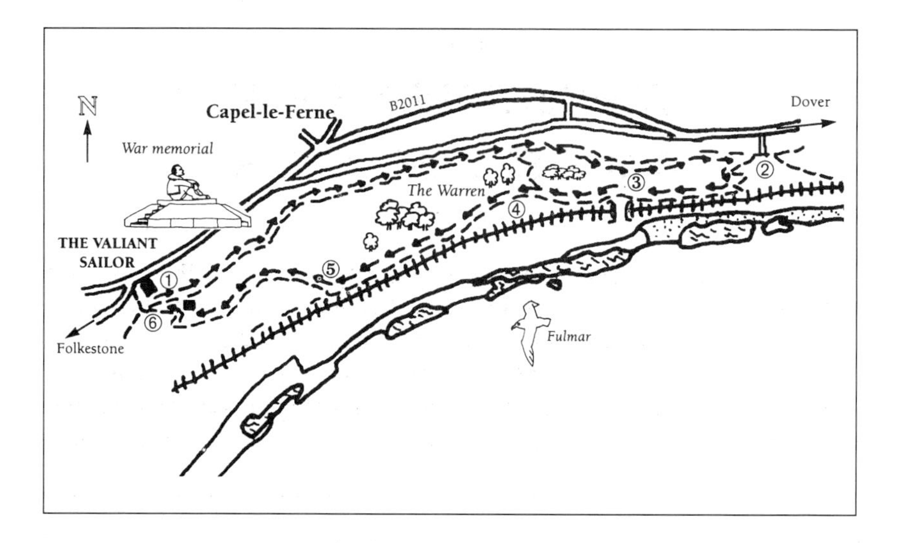

4. At the next post bear left on lower ground through the wooded Warren instead of climbing up (beware - both are signed 'Warren Fossil Trail'!) Follow the path as it leads back up onto chalky ground along the woodland edge.

Seagulls' cries remind one that the sea is close even when out of view; jackdaws screech from the clifftops; kestrels hover above; fulmars, small gull-like birds, nest on the cliff ledges or glide above.

5. At the next waymarker turn right to climb uphill through woodland and scrub (do not continue straight ahead on the Fossil Trail). Halfway up the cliff the campsite café gives a welcome break; the climb is quite arduous on a hot day. There are superb views across the bay.

6. Behind the café take the stepped path up to the clifftop. At the top turn left onto the North Downs Way and follow the path round to the right, back to the pub.

Places of Interest Nearby

You can explore the *Warren* and the adjacent *East Cliffs* further using the waymarked trails and leaflets produced by the White Cliffs Project (telephone: 01304 241806). A round Martello Tower, built on top of East Cliffs to protect against Napoleonic invasion, has been converted into a fascinating little visitor centre (telephone: 01303 242113).

WALK 18

ST MARGARET'S BAY: A WHITE CLIFF WALK

A bracing clifftop walk along these world famous chalk cliffs past lighthouses that have guided shipping in and out of Dover Harbour for centuries. Then back along an old drove road and across the springy turf of St Margaret's Down. This walk is special at all times of year, whether crisp winter walking with pink tinged skies or summer when the clifftops abound with colourful wildflowers and butterflies.

St Margaret's Bay

This stretch of coastline is nearer to France than any other part of England and the French coastline can be seen on a clear day. The area has long been looked on as the 'Gateway to England' and the white cliffs evoke fond memories for many. These high chalk cliffs have given some natural protection from invasion but there has been plenty of action here in more recent wars. The Dover Patrol laid a minefield in the Channel below during the First World War. During the Second

World War the powerful naval guns, nicknamed Winnie and Pooh, fired out to sea and the Battle of Britain, which marked the turning point, was fought in the skies above.

The Coastguard, situated on the seafront overlooking St Margaret's Bay, has the distinction of being the nearest English pub to France. In the summer the verandah cascades with hanging baskets and tubs. This is a freehouse serving a range of real ales including Boddingtons and Flowers (with a wider selection in summer), Scrumpy Jack cider and Heineken and Stella lagers. Fish and chips are the speciality of the house, as befits a seaside pub, but the menu is far more extensive. There are no special children's facilities but well-behaved children are welcome for meals and on the verandah. Dogs are allowed on the verandah. In summer the opening hours are from 11 am to 11 pm and food is served all day, including cream teas. Winter hours vary but are usually from 11 am to 2.30 pm and variable in the evenings depending on weather and trade - best to phone beforehand to confirm.

Telephone: 01304 853176.

- **HOW TO GET THERE:** Turn off the A258 between Dover and Deal, following signs to St Margaret's at Cliffe. Continue through the village and follow the narrow lane as it winds down to the sea. The Coastguard is on the right and the public car park on the left.
- **PARKING:** There is a large public car park adjacent to the pub. The pub car park itself gets extremely busy during the summer and at weekends - only leave your car there whilst walking if it is the off season and, of course, with the prior agreement of the landlord.
- **LENGTH OF THE WALK:** 5½ miles. Maps: OS Landranger 179 or Explorer 138 (GR 368444).

The Walk

1. From the Coastguard pub turn left and walk up the road away from the coast. As the road bends to the right turn left along a track signed to The Pines, following the Saxon Shore Way markers. Take the lower fork to the left at the road junction and continue past The Pines. Walk along the unmade road until you reach a path junction at the base of the downs.

2. Turn left and follow the Saxon Shore Way up to the clifftop. Turn right onto a grassy path to walk along the clifftop (this gives better views than the wider gravel track).

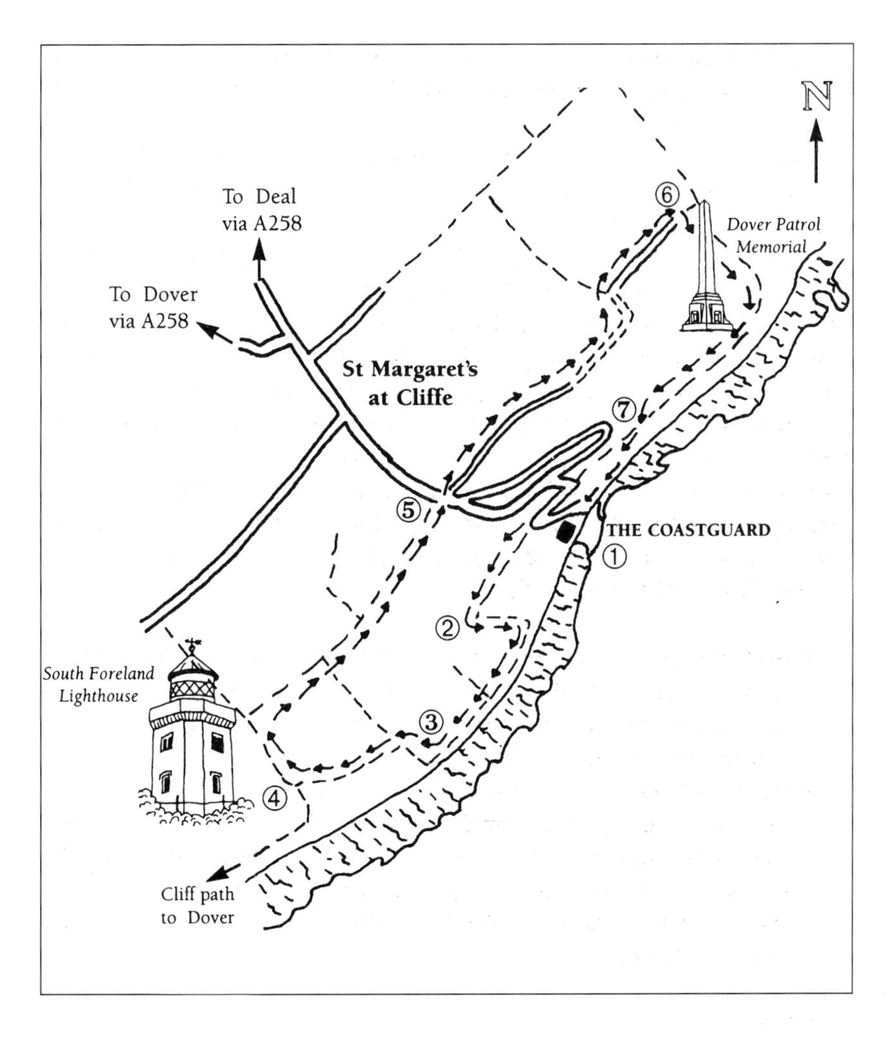

Ahead the tip of a disused lighthouse is visible and St Margaret's Windmill, which was sited on the clifftop where it could catch the wind most effectively. Built in 1928, it is Kent's most recently surviving windmill. It has a revolving cap which turns the sails towards the wind to maximise the wind power; it was used to generate electricity.

3. Follow the grassy track as it turns inland near the windmill. Then turn left to join the gravel track. Continue along the track until it meets the lane leading to South Foreland Lighthouse.

The first lighthouses were built in 1634 in response to a petition from shipowners whose ships were grounding on the dangerous offshore sandbanks. After 1905 the one nearer the cliff became too dangerous to use as the clifftop had eroded.

If you have time detour left and then right along the clifftop in front of the lighthouse for stunning views of Dover harbour.

4. Turn right in front of the lighthouse and walk to the end of the track. Where it meets Wanstone Farm drive turn right and follow this track all the way back to St Margaret's at Cliffe village. (Detour left to the village centre for shops etc, if required.)

5. Cross the road and continue straight ahead along the road opposite called The Droveway. Follow past housing for about ¾ mile and continue on the lane as it bears left and then right to Bockhill Farm. At the farm continue ahead along a droveway now a sunken path.

6. Turn right and walk along field edges out onto St Margaret's Down, with an obelisk ahead to the right.

The tall granite obelisk is a memorial to the Dover Patrol, a fleet of small boats whose brave sailors laid a minefield in the English Channel during the First World War.

At a clifftop path junction turn right past the obelisk (Blue Birds Tea Rooms are on your left) and follow the well-marked grassy path down the hillside, back to St Margaret's Bay.

7. Take the steps to the left beside a house to descend steeply to the bay. Turn right and walk along the promenade back to the Coastguard. If you prefer a less steep descent, continue ahead to the road. Turn left onto the road and follow it down to the bay.

Places of Interest Nearby

The *Bay Museum* (telephone: 01304 852764) houses exhibits showing St Margaret's Bay's role as a gateway to Europe. The *Pines Garden* opposite is open daily. *South Foreland Lighthouse* is open to the public at weekends between April and October (telephone: 01892 890651).

WALK 19

THE RIVER STOUR AT SANDWICH: WALKING THE WALLS

An easy walk along surfaced paths from the historic Quay, along the River Stour and around the old walls, giving good views of the fascinating medieval town of Sandwich.

The Admiral Owen, Sandwich

Medieval Sandwich was one of the most important ports in England, both for trade and providing warships for English kings as one of the original Cinque Ports. In its heyday it ranked as the seventh largest town in England. Many famous figures from history used the port - Thomas à Becket fleeing the wrath of Henry II, Richard the Lionheart returning from the crusades and a succession of medieval kings embarking with their armies for the wars in France. The influx of Flemish and Huguenot refugees escaping religious persecution in Europe brought improved trade links and craft skills and Sandwich's flourishing weaving trade developed. Sandwich Haven, the estuary that linked the town to the North Sea, gradually silted up and the once thriving port is now two miles from the sea. The river is still tidal and navigable to small pleasure boats but it is the stunning old buildings that tell most strongly of its former glory.

Strand Street boasts more medieval buildings than any other street in England and the choice of pub in this historic town is a fine half-timbered one on this street. The Admiral Owen dates from the 15th century when it was part of a monastery whose monks collected tolls at the nearby bridge over the Stour. Beer has long been associated with the building as the monks brewed their own ale, like many monastic orders.

The cosy alcove bar serves a tremendous selection of real ales – Greene King and a selection of guest beers from the barrel such as Archers Black Jack, Ringwood Old Thumper and Hook Norton. Theobold's Kentish or Thatcher's cider, draught Guinness, Murphy's, Strongbow and Kronenbourg are on offer. A variety of coffees also. Children are welcome to eat here but there are no special facilities. Dogs are also welcome. The opening hours are from 11 am to 11 pm on Monday to Saturday and from 12 noon to 10.30 pm on Sunday. Food is available all day on Saturday and Sunday and from 12 noon to 2.30 pm and 6 pm to 9 pm on Monday to Friday.

All food is home-cooked and prepared on the premises. An interesting range of hot dishes is available and the chalked-up menu changes regularly – starters such as moules or soup and crusty bread and hearty main meals such as beef in Guinness, lamb hot pot or mushroom, spinach and feta cheese pie. Puddings always include a home-made dessert in addition to icecreams. There is also a snack menu and sandwiches are a speciality, appropriately, as it was the Earl of Sandwich who invented the sandwich so that he could eat whilst playing at his gaming tables.

Telephone: 01304 620869.

- **HOW TO GET THERE:** From the A257 east of Canterbury, continue across the roundabout with the A256, signed to the town centre. Cross over the railway and continue into town along Strand Street. The Admiral Owen is on the corner of Strand Street near the Quay.
- **PARKING:** Plenty of parking is available on the Quay (all town car parks are free).
- **LENGTH OF THE WALK:** 3 miles. Maps: OS Landranger 179 or Explorer 150 (GR 333583).

The Walk

1. From the Admiral Owen turn left down to the river, cross the road and walk along the Quay with the river on the left.

Tolls were collected from travellers crossing the river from the days of King Canute until 1977. The imposing Barbican or gatehouse was built by Henry VIII, as part of his improved coastal defences (the threat of invasion from Europe increased following his rift from the Catholic church). Look also for Fisher Gate on the Quay, the only one of the original five town gates to survive. The Stour was much wider then and navigable for the large wooden warships which would have tied up at the quayside.

Walk to the end of the Quay and continue straight ahead (Saxon Shore Way markers) on a tarmaced path between plane trees and weeping willows.

2. Cross the river branch at a small white footbridge and follow the path round to the right. Then bear left and continue on the Stour Valley Walk as the Saxon Shore Way and Sandwich walks go off to the right.

The large expanse of reedbeds on the left provides homes for reed warblers and other waterbirds. The fertile flat land surrounding the river has been drained to allow arable crops to grow.

3. Cross the footbridge over New Cut and turn right along the road, leaving the Stour Valley Walk. (For a longer walk just continue on along the Stour Valley Walk, across the golf course to the coast.) Follow the road, with the golf course on the left and arable fields on the right, until you reach the golf club buildings on the left.

These raised earthen seawalls and cuts are part of the measures taken to reclaim the marshland for grazing when the estuary silted up.

4. Take the footpath right, signed for the Saxon Shore Way, back across fields towards Sandwich. Cross the white footbridge over New Cut and then go across the field to walk alongside Vigo Sprong (another drainage channel) on the left. Rejoin the main path back towards the Quay.

5. Turn left by a playground and walk alongside The Bulwarks, the first section of the walk around the old town walls.

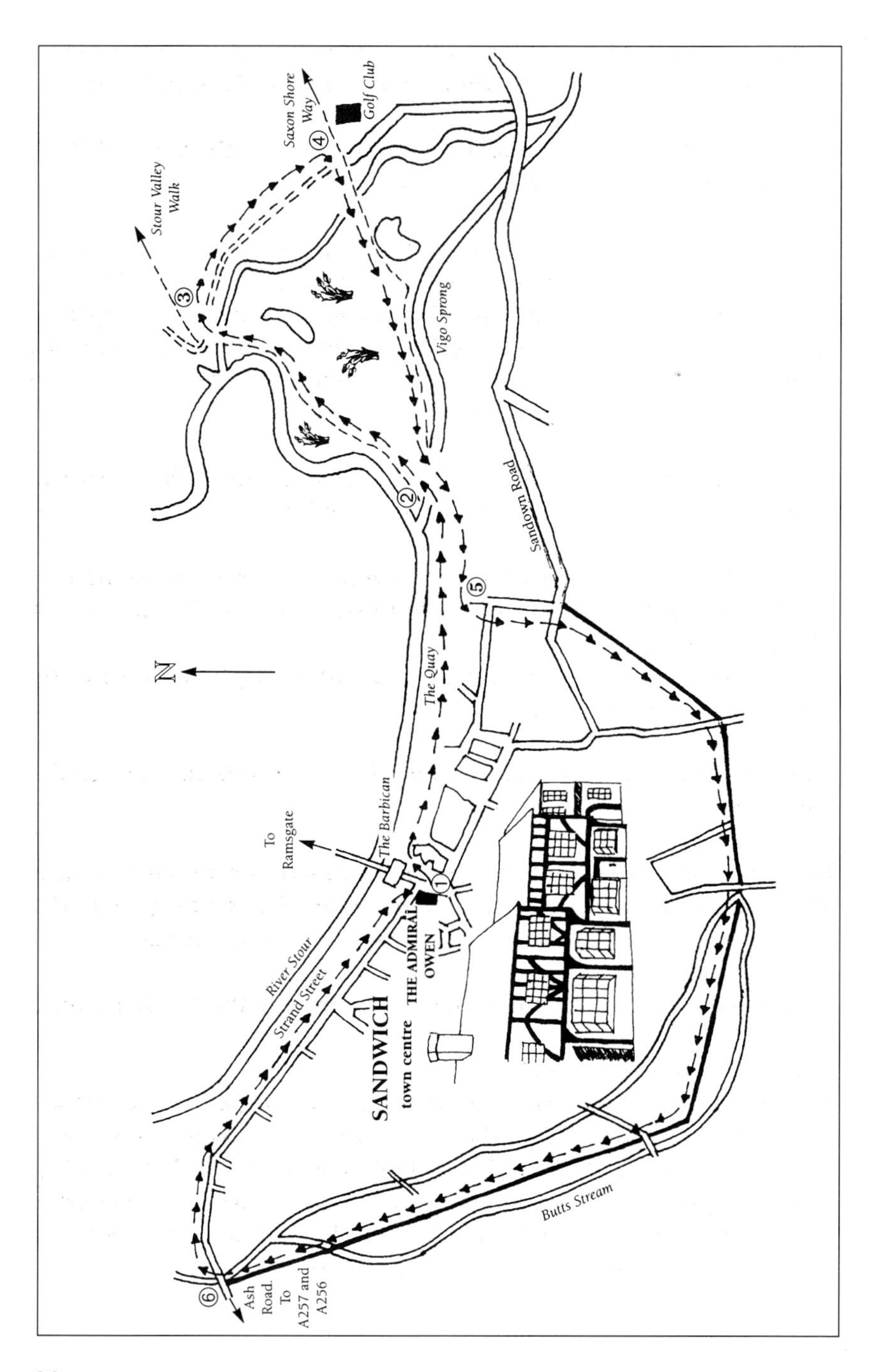
Saxon Shore Way
Golf Club
Stour Valley Walk
Vigo Sprong
Sandown Road
N
The Quay
The Barbican
To Ramsgate
River Stour
Strand Street
SANDWICH
town centre
THE ADMIRAL OWEN
Butts Stream
Ash Road. To A257 and A256
1
2
3
4
5
6

Richard II ordered the building of these stone walls to protect the town from the constant threat of raids and invasion in the Middle Ages.

Cross the road and continue straight ahead on the path along Mill Wall. Continue along the ramparts around the town.

This raised walk gives a good view of the old town. Firstly of the parish church tower behind the houses edging Mill Wall, and further on the town bowling green flanked by attractive houses. Different church spires are visible as you look back to town from various points and there are good views down winding lanes edged with tightly packed cottages and houses.

Cross New Road (the site of New Gate) and walk alongside the stream on Rope Walk, then across Woodnesborough Road.

This section of the walls was used for making ships' ropes. Hemp was spun, tarred, stranded and then laid into ropes up to 300 yards long along these ramparts.

Look for the lovely stone almshouses on the right with a square oast behind at Loop Street.

Then continue along the final stretch of walls, The Butts, back to the lower end of Strand Street.

The Butts, once used in Tudor times as an archery practice field, is leafy and pleasant with rows of limes and planes edging the path and weeping willows nearer the stream that runs alongside.

6. Turn right and walk along Strand Street, back to the Admiral Owen.

Places of Interest Nearby

In the town is *Sandwich Guildhall Museum* (telephone: 01304 617197) and on the road to the A256/A257 roundabout is the *White Mill Folk Museum* in an old windmill (telephone: 01304 612076). *Richborough Castle* – the remains of a large Roman fort that once protected the coastline and was a base for Roman garrisons – is to the north of the town (telephone: 01304 612013).

WALK 20

BROADSTAIRS: SEACLIFFS AND SMUGGLERS

The circuit starts with a bracing clifftop walk to Foreness Point with good views of the dramatic cliff formations around the bays. If the tide is out you can come back along the foreshore and explore the fascinating chalk rockpools. If preferred you can return via Northdown Park and Reading Street, a pretty hamlet that was once the haunt of smugglers, and the North Foreland Lighthouse.

Kingsgate Bay

The Broadstairs area is very busy in the summer but this walk also makes a refreshing autumn and winter outing when the crowds are absent. At any time of year a short stretch along the cliffs and a return along the shore is an ideal trip for families and the Captain Digby, the starting and finishing point, has excellent children's facilities.

This flint pub was originally built as a folly by Lord Holland - one of several erected in the 18th century by this eccentric lord on the clifftops around here! It was originally used as a place to entertain his guests and the present pub is almost identical to the original. Smuggling was rife all along this coastline and smugglers reputedly used the large subterranean caverns that ran from the inn down to the shore.

The Captain Digby is spacious with lots of different seating areas, some with superb views across the bay. Children enjoy the garden and outdoor play area; also the indoor play area for which there is a small charge. Among the varied dishes on offer are battered cod, steak and ale pie, roast peppercorn chicken plus hot and spicy specials such as chilli and rice, beef madras curry or Caribbean fruity vegetable curry. Chargrill meals including garlic and herb chicken breast, sirloin steak and the Captain's Grill are also available. There is a children's menu too. The pub is open all day from 11 am seven days a week.

Telephone: 01843 867764.

- **HOW TO GET THERE:** Take the B2052 north from Broadstairs to Joss Bay. The Captain Digby is on the right just past Kingsgate Bay.
- **PARKING:** Spaces are limited in summer when the area gets very busy. Walkers may leave their cars in the pub car park provided they buy a parking ticket (£10) which is redeemable against food and drinks. Alternatively, there is a car park at Joss Bay.
- **LENGTH OF THE WALK:** 4 miles. Maps: OS Landranger 179 or Explorer 150 (GR 395706).

THE WALK

1. From the front entrance of the pub overlooking the bay turn left and follow the path out onto the clifftop.

The crumbled ruin on the left is Neptune's Tower, another of Lord Holland's creations, built as a replica of Deal Castle around an ancient chalk watchtower. The chalk tower has long since crumbled but the flint base remains.

Bear left along the clifftop along the path (unless you wish to descend onto the beach if the tide allows). Follow the clifftop path, passing a path down to Botany Bay, opposite Dolphin Close.

Botany Bay may have got its name from Botany Bay in Australia to which captured smugglers may have been deported. The rocks in the

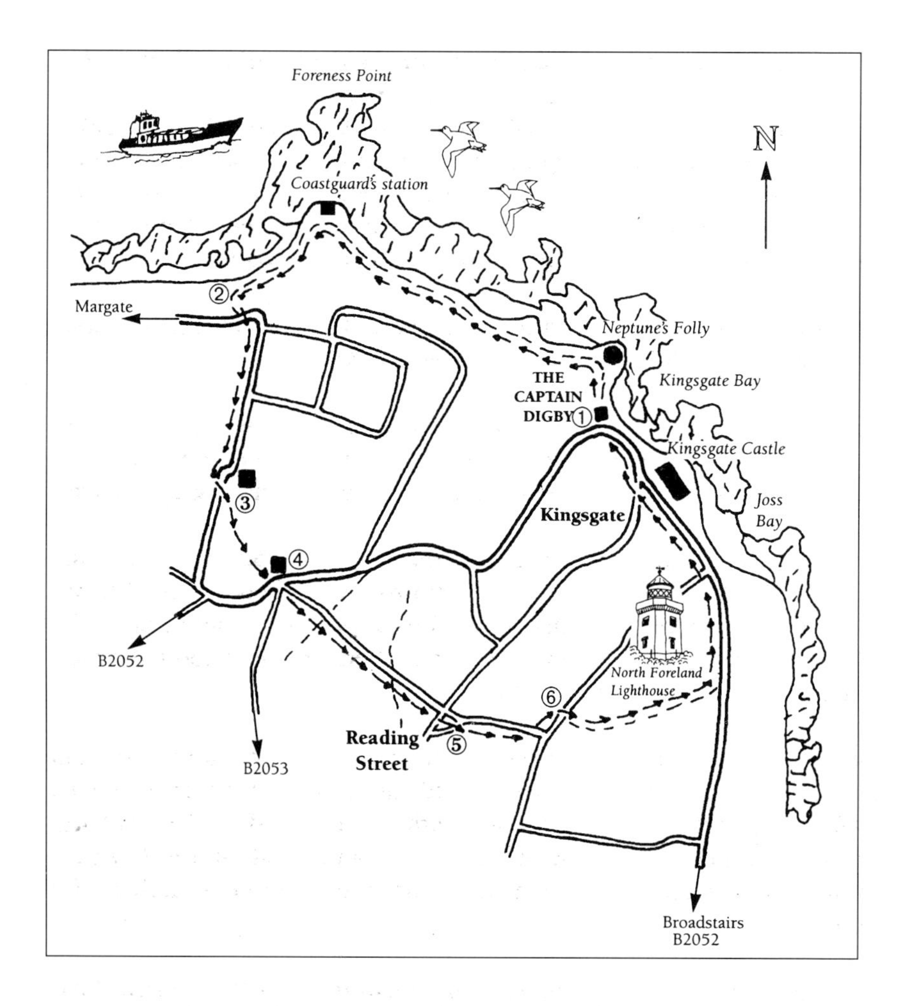

bay are used as a high tide roost by large numbers of seabirds.

Keep going along the clifftop path across the rough grassland and along the headland to the coastguard station at Foreness Point.

The chalk is relatively soft and easily eroded which has resulted in these cliffs, dramatic stacks, and, on the beach, the reef-like chalk platforms.

The cliffs and rocky shore attract many birds. The black and white oystercatcher and smaller ringed plover with its distinctive dark neckband can be seen on the shore all year round. Fulmars, small gull-like birds, nest in the cliffs and in the colder weather a host of waders and wildfowl come to overwinter here.

In summer the cliffs are colourful with wildflowers. Pink valerian and cream wild carrot grow in crevices on the cliff face. Yellow-flowered alexanders, a tall celery-like plant known as 'poor man's asparagus', and chalk loving plants including scented marjoram and thyme cover the clifftops, attracting lots of butterflies.

Follow the clifftop path past the coastguard station and the golf course, towards the landing stage and summer café/kiosk.

2. Turn left just before the kiosk and walk alongside the golf course to the road. Turn left along the road, Palm Bay Avenue, and then turn right onto Princess Margaret's Avenue. Walk to the end of this residential road.

3. Cross the road and enter Northdown Park beside Cliftonville Library. Walk across the park to Northdown House, now Thanet District Council offices. Turn left in the car park and walk through the formal gardens. Go through the gate and then turn right and follow the drive round to the left to join the road.

4. Cross the road and turn left. At the road junction take the second road to the right, Reading Street Road (no pavement but fairly quiet). After a short distance take the footpath into the field on the right and follow the path parallel with the road. Continue along the footpath until it rejoins the road beside allotments and continue walking to the crossroads.

5. Cross over and continue straight ahead towards the church. Bear left along the road, passing Rimpton Court. Turn left at the T junction onto Elmwood Avenue.

The pretty village of Reading Street was a small farming hamlet one hundred years ago. It has, however, had a much stormier past as many of the residents were involved in smuggling at one time and raids by the Revenue were frequent. Look for the 'barrel' house signs on some of the flint cottages. Rosemary Cottage, set back on the left beyond the Old School House, used to have a lantern hanging outside, reputedly to warn smugglers on the beach that the village was clear of Revenue men for unloading booty.

6. Take the footpath on the right just before the derestricted sign. Walk past riding stables on the left and at the end turn left onto a path clearly leading up to North Foreland Lighthouse. Old convent buildings can be seen on the hillside to the right.

The beautifully maintained North Foreland Lighthouse is the oldest lighthouse still in use in England. A primitive beacon was in place by 1500 and its light guided the ships sailing against the Spanish Armada. The present building was begun in 1791 and the light was initially an open fire fuelled by coal, then an oil lamp, until in the late 1930s it was converted to electricity.

Turn left and walk along the road in front of the lighthouse down into Joss Bay on the pavement.

There are good views out to sea and Kingsgate Castle is prominent – yet another folly of Lord Holland's, originally built along the lines of a Welsh fortress!

Farmers used to gather seaweed and collect flints for building walls and houses from the beach. They cut paths into the cliffs, known as seagates, to give access to the shore. It is widely thought that Joss Bay was named after the notorious smuggler Joss Snelling, but it is more likely to have been named after Joss Farm whose tenants collected seaweed there.

Walk along the edge of the golf course and turn right, back onto the road, by Kingsgate Castle. Turn left and walk along the road to reach the Captain Digby.

A pitched battle took place on Kingsgate cliffs below the Captain Digby between Revenue men and a smuggling gang in March 1769. The notorious 'Callis Court Gang' were betrayed to the Revenue and ambushed whilst unloading their contraband.

Places of Interest Nearby

Broadstairs, to the south, retains some of its genteel Victorian air. Charles Dickens' holiday home, Bleak House, is open in the summer (Tourist Information Centre telephone: 01843 862242). *Margate*, to the west of Foreness Point, is a bigger resort with all the usual facilities (Tourist Information Centre telephone: 01843 220241).